VIKRAMA AND URVASI

OR

THE HERO AND THE NYMPH

A DRAMA

TRANSLATED FROM THE ORIGINAL

SANSCRIT

VIKRAMA AND URVASI

OR

THE HERO AND THE NYMPH

A DRAMA

TRANSLATED FROM THE ORIGINAL

SANSCRIT

BY

HORACE HAYMAN WILSON, ESQ.

Secretary to the Asiatic Society of Bengal, &c.

GYAN

Published by

Gyan Publishing House
5, Ansari Road
Daryaganj, New Delhi-110002
Phone: 011-47034999, 9811692060
E-mail: books@gyanbooks.com

Distribution Network
gyanbooks.com
India, USA, Canada, UK, Australia, France

ISBN : 978-81-212-2750-6 (HB)
First Published, 1826

2nd Impression 2021

Printed at: Gyan Press, Delhi.

Vikrama and Urvasi
Translated by: Horace Hayman Wilson

VIKRAMA AND URVASI,

OR

THE HERO AND THE NYMPH.

A DRAMA

TRANSLATED FROM THE ORIGINAL

SANSCRIT,

BY

HORACE HAYMAN WILSON, ESQ.

Secretary to the Asiatic Society of Bengal, &c.

CALCUTTA:

V. HOLCROFT, ASIATIC PRESS,

No. 3, Council House Street.

1826.

VIKRAMA AND URVASI

OR

THE HERO AND THE NYMPH.

VIKRAMA AND URVASI,

THE HERO AND THE NYMPH.

PREFACE.

The drama of VIKRAMA and URVASI is one of the three plays attributed to KALIDASA, already advantageously known to the western world, as the Author of *Sakuntalá*—the introductory observation of the Manager in the prelude is our evidence to this effect, and it is corroborated by the correspondence of these two compositions, in many of their characteristic merits and defects: the subject of each is taken from heroic mythology, and a royal demigod and nymph of more than human mould are the hero and heroine of either; there is the same vivacity of description, and tenderness of feeling in both; the like delicate beauty in the thoughts, and extreme elegance in the style: it may be difficult to decide to which the palm belongs but the story of the present play is perhaps more skilfully woven, and the incidents rise out of each other more naturally than in Sakuntalá, while on the other hand, there is perhaps no one personage in it so interesting as the heroine of that drama.

Although however there is no reason to doubt that this play is the work of the same hand as that translated by Sir Wm. Jones, the concurrence does not throw any further light upon the date or history of the author: we can only infer from the observance of the same chaste style of composition, and the absence of any forced construction, or offensive conceits, that they are both the production of a period anterior to the reign of BHOJA, when *his* KALIDAS, a man of fancy and taste, could descend to write a whole poem, the *Nalodaya*, for instance, in a strain of verbal paltering and a succession of jingling sounds.

The richness of the *Prákrit* in this play both in structure and in its metrical code, is very remarkable: a very great portion, especially of the fourth act, is in this language, and in that act also a considerable variety of metre is introduced as will be hereafter more particularly noticed: it is clear therefore that this form of Sanscrit must have been highly cultivated long before the play was written, and this might lead us to doubt whether the composition can bear so remote a date as the reign of VIKRAMADITYA. (56. *B. C.*) It is yet rather uncertain whether the classical language of Hindu literature had at that time received so high a polish as appears in the present drama, and still less therefore could the descendants have been exquisitely refined, if the parent were comparatively rude. We can scarcely conceive that the cultivation of *Prakrit* preceded that of Sanscrit, when we advert to the principles on which the former seems to be evolved from the latter, but it must be confessed that the relation between Sanscrit and *Prákrit* has been hitherto very imperfectly investigated, and is yet far from being understood.

It may be thought some argument for the comparative antiquity of the present drama that it tells the story of PURURAVAS very differently from the Puránas, in several of which it may be fo und: we may suppose therefore that the play preceded those works, as had it been subsequently composed the poet would either spontaneously, or in deference to sacred authority have adhered more closely to the Pauranic legend: thedifference n the Puránas also indicates that corruption of taste which we cannot hesitate regarding as the product of more modern and degenerate days.

The Loves of PURURAVAS and URVASI are related in various Puránas: the following is the story as it appears in the *Vishnu Purána* in which and in the *Padma,** it is more fully and connectedly detailed than perhaps in any other composition of the same class.

URVASI, the *Apsaras*, or one of the nymphs of heaven so named, having incurrea the displeasure of MITRA and VARUNA was sentenced by them to become the consort of a mortal, and in consequence of this curse she became enamoured of the king PURURAVAS, the son of BUDHA and ILA. Forgetting her celestial duties, and foregoing the delights of *Swerga*, she introduced herself to the monarch, and her charms did not fail to make the due impression on his heart. She was delicately and symmetrically formed, was graceful in her gestures and fascinating in her manners; her voice was music, her countenance was dressed in smiles, and her beauty was such as might enchant the world; no wonder

* It is the subject also of a work of some length in Telugu —called the Kaviraja Manoranjanam or Pururava Charitram composed by *Avyaya*—the minister of a petty prince in the Dekhin, the Raja of *Condavir*, this story follows the Puranas but with some differences.

therefore that PURURAVAS was at once inspired with fervent love: confiding in his rank and renown, the king did not hesitate to propose a matrimonial alliance to the nymph of heaven: she was nothing loth, but had not the power to comply, without previously exacting the bridegroom's consent to two conditions. PURURAVAS hesitated not to accede to the stipulations.

URVASI had with her two pet rams, creatures of heavenly and illusive natures, and one of her conditions was that the king should take these animals under his own charge, and guard against their being ever carried away by fraud or force. The other stipulation was, that the nymph was never to behold the person of the king, divested of his rainment. On the ready accession of PURURAVAS to these terms, URVASI became his bride, and they dwelt together in the forest of *Chaitraratha*, near *Alaká* the capital of KUVERA, for sixty one* years, in perfect happiness and undiminished affection.

The absence of URVASI was very soon felt in the upper sphere, and the inhabitants of *Swerga* found their enjoyments stale and unprofitable, no longer heightened by the agreeable manners and entertaining society of the nymph. The whole body of *Apsarasas, Siddhas, Gandharbas,* and other tenants of Indra's heaven, regretted her loss, and determined to attempt her recovery as soon as the period of her exile, as denounced by the imprecation, should have expired. When this period arrived, they deputed some of the *Gandharbas* on the expedition, who undertook to bring about the violation of the terms on which the alliance of the

* This is however a mere moment in the extravagant duration of the life of PURURAVAS according to the *Puránas*: there is nothing of the kind in the play.

king and the nymph depended: with this intent they entered the sleeping chamber of the monarch, and carried off one of the rams: the bleat of the animal woke URVASI, who echoed its cries with her lamentations, and aroused the prince. Apprehensive however of appearing before his bride, undressed, PURURAVAS hesitated to pursue the thief, and thus incurred the angry reproaches of his spouse for his indifference to her loss. Presently the *Gandharbas* bore away the second ram, and the grief of URVASI was afresh excited; the king's indignation also could no longer be restrained, and determined to pursue and punish the ravishers he leaped naked out of bed, trusting that the darkness of night would screen him from the eye of his consort. This was what his enemies desired, and he was no sooner off the couch, than a vivid flash of lightning revealed him to view, and put an end to his union with the nymph of *Swerga*. URAVSI immediately disappeared, accompanying the *Gandharbas* to the halls of INDRA.

When PURURAVAS was conscious of his loss, his grief was so intense, that it affected his intellects, and he long wandered frantic over the world in quest of his bride—after many years had elapsed he came to a lake in *Kurukshetra* where he found several Nymphs sporting on the bank; amongst them was URVASI: recognising her at once he ran to her and with wild energy implored her return; the Nymph however was no longer disposed, even if she had been permitted, to comply with his wishes, and was deaf to all his entreaties, and at last she succeeded in convincing him of the unreasonableness of his solicitations, and prevailed on him to resume his station, and the duties of a King, engaging on those terms to pay him an annual visit—PURURAVAS, however reluctantly, was compelled to submit, and returned sorrowfully but composed to his capital: his annual interviews with URVASI were punctually repeated and the fruit of this intercourse was the birth of six Sons* AYUS, DHIMAN AMAVASU, VISWAVASU, SATAYU and SRUTAYU, who were the progenitors of the lunar race of kings.

The occasional interviews with his bride granted to PURURAVAS were far from satisfying his desires, and he still sighed for the permanent enjoyment of her society: the *Gandharbas* at last pitying his distress, engaged to promote his reunion with the nymph, and sent the king a brazier charged with fire, with which they directed him to perform a sacrifice in the forest, to attain the gratification of all his wishes. The king repaired to the woods, but reflecting that he had quitted URVASI in order to celebrate this rite, giving up the substance for the shadow, he returned to seek the nymph, leaving the vessel of fire in the thicket. Not finding his consort he again directed his steps to the forest, but there the brazier was gone, and on the spot where it had stood, a *Sami*† and *Aswattha*‡ tree had sprung up. After a little consideration PURURAVAS broke a branch from either tree, and carried them back to the palace, where reciting the *Gáyatri*§ and rubbing the sticks together, he generated fire with the friction: this primeval fire he divided into three portions and with them he performed various sacrifices and oblations until he obtained the rank of a *Gandharba*

* All this part of the story, *Urvasi's* loss and recovery, and the birth of *Ayus*, are totally different in the play.

† Mimosa Suma.

‡ Religious Fig.

§ The holiest verse of the Vedas.

and being elevated to the regions of *Swerga,* there enjoyed the constant society of his beloved Urvasi.*

The latter circumstances of this legend seem to indicate the introduction of fire worship into India by Pururavas, considered as a historical personage.† There may have been some old tradition to that effect, whence the *Pauranic* writers derived the ground work of their fable, but it is not noticed in the play, neither is any allusion made to it in the version of this story in another work in which it is found, the *Vrihat Kathá,* which differs in many particulars from both the play and the *Purána.* The story there however is very concisely narrated, and the author has clearly taken merely the personages and course of the fable, from what was currently known, and givenhis own colouring to the incidents. It adds therefore nothing to the history of the narrative, and may be either anterior or subsequent to the forms in which it is now presented to English readers. Another authority however, the *Matsya Purána,* tells the story more agreeably to the tenor of the drama, as follows:

"When a year had elapsed, the divine *Tárá* bore a son of surpassing splendour, arrayed in celestial raiment of a yellow colour, and richly decorated with heavenly gems: from his youth he was versed in regal duties and was so skilled in the training of elephants that he taught the art, and acquired the appellation of *Gajavedhaka.* The Gods being assem-

* The play makes no allusion to these incidents, closing with the appearance of the elder son, *Ayus*

† The three fires are the *Gárhapatya* or perpetual fire maintained by a householder, the *Ahavaniya* or consecrated fire taken from the preceding and prepared for receiving oblations, and the *Dakshinágni* fire taken from either of the former and placed towards the South.

bled at the mansion of her husband, *Vrihaspati*, to perform the rites due to his birth, enquired of *Tárá* whose son he was, and with much reluctance she acknowledged the Royal *Soma* was his father. *Soma* therefore took the boy, and named him *Budha*, and gave him dominion on the earth, and inaugurated him supreme over the world. *Brahmá* and the rest conferred upon him the dignity of a planetary power and then took their departure.

The holy *Budha* begot by *Ilá* a son, who performed by his own might a hundred Aswamedhas. He was named PURURAVAS and was revered by all worlds. He worshipped *Vishnu* on the peaks of Himálaya, and thence became the monarch of the seven fold earth. KESI and myriads of *Daityas* fell before his prowess, and URVASI fascinated by his personal graces, became his bride.

Virtue, *Wealth*, and *Desire*, once paid this monarch a visit, curious to ascertain which of them held the first place in his esteem. The king received them with respect but payed to *Virtue* his profoundest homage. *Wealth* and *Desire* were offended by the preference shewn to their companion. *Wealth* denounced a curse upon him, that Avarice should occasion his fall, and *Desire* declared that he should be separated from his bride, and on that account suffer distraction in the forest of Kumára on the Gandhamádana mountain; but *Virtue* declared he should enjoy a long and pious life, that his descendants should continue to multiply, as long as the Sun and Moon endured, and should ever enjoy dominion of the earth—After this the divinities disappeared.

PURURAVAS was in the habit of paying a visit to *Indra* every day. Having ascended his car, accompanying the Sun in his southern course, he beheld on one occasion the Demon

Kesi seize and carry off the nymphs *Chitralekhá* and Urvasi. The king attacked the demon, and destroyed him with the shaft of *Váyu,* by which he not only rescued the nymphs, but established *Indra* on his throne, which the Demon had endangered—for this service *Indra* repaid the monarch with his friendship, and gave him additional power, splendor, and glory.

Having invited the king to a festival at which was represented the celebrated story of *Lakshmi's* election of a husband, the invention of Bharata, Indra commanded Menaka, Rembha and Urvasi to perform their respective parts. Urvasi who represented *Lakshmi,* being engrossed by admirration of the king, forgot what she had to enact, and thereby incurred the high displeasure of the sage, who sentenced her to separation from the Prince on earth, and condemned her to pine fifty five years transformed to a Vine, until restored to the regrets of Pururavas. Urvasi having made the King her Lord, resided with him, and after the term of the curse had expired bore him eight sons—*Ayu, Dhrirháyu, Aswáyu, Dhanáyu, Dhritimán, Vasu, Divijata,* and *Sátayu* all endowed with more than human power."

This story is evidently that of the play, although related less in detail, and with a few variations according to Pauranic taste—but it is clear that it is either derived from a common source with the narration of the drama, or which is not improbable, that it has borrowed from the latter its general complexion. The nature of the relation which exists between the fiction as it appears in the Drama, and in the *Puránas,* our readers will be able to appreciate for themselves after perusal of the former.

DRAMATIS PERSONÆ.

OF THE PRELUDE.

MANAGER. ACTOR.

OF THE PLAY.

MEN.

Purúravas.—King of *Pratishthána.*

Ayus.—The son of *Purúravas.*

Mánava.—The *Vidúshaka* and confidential companion of the king.

Chitrasena.—King of the *Gandherbas* the attendants on *Indra.*

Náreda.—The divine sage, the son of *Brahmá.*

Chamberlain.

A Forester.

Paila
Gálava. } Two disciples of the sage *Bharata.*

WOMEN.

Urvasí.—An *Apsaras* or nymph of *Indra's* heaven.

Chitralekhá.—Another nymph, her friend.

Sahajanyá
Rembhá
Menaká. } Nymphs.*

* According to the *Kasi Khand* there are thirty-five millions of these nymphs, but only one thousand and sixty are the principal—of these however not more than five or six are the subject of Pauranic or poetical narrations—or *Urvasí,*

Ausinarí.—The queen of *Purúravas* and daughter of the king of *Kásí* or *Benares.*

Nipuniká.—One of her attendants.

PERSONS SPOKEN OF.

Indra.—The chief of all the inferior Deities, and Sovereign of *Swerga* or Paradise.

Késí.—A *Daitya* or *Titan* an enemy of the Gods.

Bharata.—A holy sage the inventor of dramatic composition.

Guards.—Nymphs &c.

Scene in the First Act the Peaks of the *Himálaya;* in the second and third, the palace of *Purúravas* at *Pratishthána;* in the fourth, the forest of *Akalusha,* and in the fifth again at the palace.

(Time —Uncertain.)

Menaká, Rambhá, Tillottamá, and *Alambushá.* In their birth and denomination, they offer some analogy to the Goddess *Aphrodite:* like her they arose from the sea, and as her name is referred to *Aphros* foam or spray, so that of the *Apsarases,* is from *Ap* water and *Sara* who moves—their origin is thus related in the first book of the *Rámáyana.*

Then from the agitated deep upsprung
The legion of *Apsarasas,* so named
That to the watery element they owed
Their being. Myriads were they born, and all
In vesture heavenly clad, and heavenly gems:
Yet more divine their native semblance, rich
With all the gifts of grace, and youth, and beauty.
A train innumerous followed: yet thus fair
Nor God nor Demon sought their wedded love:
Thus *Rághava* they still remain—their charms
The common treasure of the host of heaven.

VIKRAMA AND URVASI.

PRELUDE.

ENTER THE MANAGER.

May that* *Siva* protect you who is attainable by devotion and faith ;† who is the sole male of the ‡ Vedánta, § spread through all space, to whom alone the name of || Lord is applicable, and who is sought with suppressed breath ¶ by those who covet final emancipation.**

* The term used in the text is *Sthánu* a name of SIVA from *Sthá* to stay or be, the existent or eternal.

† *Bhakti* faith and *Yoga* the practice of abstract meditation.

‡ The *Eka purusha*, the active instrument in creation.

§ The theological or metaphysical portion of the Vedas.

|| *Iswara*, which is derived from Isha, to have power, or Asu to pervade—in the latter case the vowel is changed.

¶ The exercise of Pránáyama or breathing through either nostril alternately and then closing both during the repetition mentally of certain formulæ.

** Inferior enjoyment in heaven is not an object of desire to the more enthusiastic of the Hindus, as it is but finite, and after its cessation, the individual is born again in the world, and exposed to the calamities of a frail existence—the great aim of devotion is union with the supreme and universal spirit, in which case the soul no more assumes a perishable shape : the character of this benediction corresponds with that of *Sakun-*

Man. (*Looking off the stage.*) Ho, *Márisha** come hither.

ENTER ACTOR.

Act. Here am I Sir.

Man. Many assemblies have witnessed the compositions of former dramatic Bards.† I therefore propose to exhibit one not hitherto represented, the drama‡ of *Vikrama* and *Urvasi.* Desire the company to be ready to do justice to their respective parts.

Act. I shall Sir.

Man. I have now only to request the audience that they will listen to this work of *Kálidása* with attention and kindness, in consideration of its subject and respect for the Author.§

(*Behind the Scenes.*)

Help, help, if in the middle sky,
A friend be found—to aid us fly.

talá and both indicate the author's belonging to that modification of the Hindu faith in which the abstract deism of the Vedánta is qualified by identifying the supreme, invisible, and inappreciable spirit with a delusive form which was the person of *Rudra or Siva.* The Brahmans of the South and West are mostly of this sect—and whatever *Sankara Swami* may have taught, it is that of his descendants the Das-námi Gosains. The sect is probably the oldest of all now existing in India.

* A term by which it is proper to address one of the principal performers.

† *Kálidas* is therefore not the oldest dramatic writer.

‡ The *Trotaka* a drama in five, eight, or nine acts, the characters of which are mixed or heavenly and human : see the introduction.

§ The original may be so understood although it is not quite clear. Pranayishu dákshinyád, yadi vá sadvastu purusha bahumánah—srinuta manobhiravahitaik kriyam imam Kalidásasya. It is of little consequence, except that in the sense preferred it indicates the fame of the author to be established when this piece was written.

Man. What sounds are these in the air, that like the plaintive bleat of lambs, break in upon my speech: was it the murmur of the Bee or *Koïl's* distant song, or do the Nymphs of heaven as they pass above, warble their celestial strains—Ah no—it is the cry of distress The fair creation of the saint, the friend of NARA, URVASI, has been carried off by a demon on her return from the halls of the Sovereign of *Kailása** and her sisters are invoking some friendly power to their aid. [*Exit.*

ACT I.

SCENE FIRST.

PART OF THE HIMALAYA RANGE OF MOUNTAINS.

ENTER *in the Air a Troop of Apsarasas or Nymphs of Heaven.*

Nymphs. Help, help if any friend be nigh
To aid the daughters of the sky.

ENTER *Purúravas*† *in a heavenly car driven by his Charioteer.*

Pur. Suspend your cries, in me behold a friend,
Purúravas, returning from the sphere
Of the wide glancing sun, command my aid
And tell me, what you dread.

* Kuvera, the God of wealth, whose capital *Alaká* is supposed to be situated on mount *Kailása.*

† *Purúravas* is a king of high descent being sprung by his mother *Ilá* from the sun, and his father *Budha* from the moon, being the grandson of the latter and great grandson of the former—his origin is ultimately derived from Brahma thus.

BRAHMA.

Daksha, — Atri,
Aditi* Kasyapa, — Soma,
Viwaswat the sun,
Vaiwaswat,
Ila, — Budha* Ila,
Pururavas.

Rembhá. A demon's violence.

Pur. What violence presumes the fiend to offer.

Menaká. Great king it thus has chanced: we measured back
Our steps from an assembly of the Gods
Held in* *Kuvera's* hall—before us stepped
The graceful *Urvasi,* the Nymph whose charms
Defeated *Indra's* stratagems† and shamed
The loveliness of *Sri*‡—the brightest ornament
Of heaven: when on our path the haughty *Dánava,*
Kési, the monarch of the golden city||
Sprang fierce and bore the struggling nymph away.

Pur. Which path pursued the wretch.

Sahajanyá. 'Tis yonder.

Pur. Banish your fears.
I go to rescue and restore your friend.

Rembhá. The act is worthy of your high descent.

Pur. Where wait you my return.

Rembhá Here—on this peak
The towering *Hemakúta.*§

Pur. (*To the Charioteer.*) Bend our course
To yonder point, and urge the rapid steeds
To swiftest flight—'tis done; before the car
Like vollied dust the scattering clouds divide;
The whirling wheel deceives the dazzled eye
And double round the axle seems to circle:
The waving chowrie on the steed's broad brow

* The God of Riches.

† See the note in page 20.

‡ The wife of Vishnu goddess of prosperity and beauty.

|| *Hiranyapur,* is the name in the text.

§ The golden or Snowy Peak.

Points backward, motionless as in a picture;
And backward streams the banner from the breeze
We meet—immoveable*—We should outstrip
The flight of *Vainatéya*† and must surely
O'ertake the ravisher. [*Exeunt.*

Rembhá. Now Sisters on, and blithely seek
The golden mountain's glittering peak;
Secure the king extracts the dart
That rankles in each anxious heart.

Menaká. We need not fear: his arm can quell
The mightiest of the sons of hell.
What makes he here—but aid to bring
From mortal realms to *Swerga's* king;
And is not to his valour given
Command o'er all the hosts of heaven. (*they proceed.*

Rembhá. Joy, Sisters, joy, the king advances;
High o'er yon ridgy rampart dances
The deer-emblazoned banner—See
The heavenly car rolls on; 'tis he.

* A very similar description, but less picturesque and just, occurs in the beginning of Sakuntalá, and the truth of it is rendered less striking by a loose translation. Sir William Jones translates Nishkampa Chámara Sikhá—"they tossed their manes" when it means "their manes and the Chowries on their heads are unagitated"—that is they point against the wind without waving, a predicate much more indicative of a rapid advance against the breeze than the undulation of either. The Chámari or Chowrie—the white bushy tail of the Tibet Cow, fixed on a gold or ornamented shaft, rose from between the ears of the horse like the Plume of the War horse of Chivalry—the banner or banneret with the device of the Chief rose at the back of the Car—sometimes several little triangular flags were mounted on its sides.

† Garura the son of Vinatá.

ENTER *Purúravas in his car slowly; Urvasí in the car fainting, supported by Chitralekhá.*

Chitr. Dear friend revive.

Pur. Fair nymph resume your courage:
Still wields the thunderer his bolt, and guards
The triple world from harm; the foes of heaven
Are put to flight—why cherish this alarm
When its just cause is o'er; unclose those lids—
The lotus opens when the night retires.

Chitr. Alas her sighs alone declare her conscious.

Pur. Soft as the flower the timid heart not soon
Forgoes its fears—The scarf that veils her bosom
Hides not its flutterings, and the panting breast,
Seems as it felt the wreath of heavenly blossoms
Weigh too oppressively.

Chitr. Revive my friend
This weakness ill becomes a nymph of heaven.

Pur. Have patience—she recovers, though but faintly;
So gently steals the moon upon the night
Retiring tardily—so peeps the flame
Of evening fires through smoky wreaths; and thus,
The Ganges slowly clears her troubled wave,
Engulphs the ruin that the tumbling bank
Had hurled athwart her agitated course,
And flows a clear and stately stream again*

* The idea in the last four lines is somewhat expanded, to convey more distinctly to European readers what one-fourth of their number would at once convey to those acquainted with the subject of the description: the original lines are exceedingly sweet and beautiful.

Chitr. Awake dear friend, the enemies of heaven
Are baffled in despair.

Urv. (*Reviving.*) By *Indra's* prowess.

Chitr. By prowess not inferior to *Mahendra's*:
By this most holy Prince* *Purúravas.*

Urv. (*Looking at Purúravas; then apart.*)
What thanks I owe the *Dánava.*

Pur. (*After looking at Urvasí, then apart.*) What marvel,
The Nymphs celestial blushed with humbled charms,
When to rebuke their wantonness, the sage
Willed that this wondrous beauty should appear.
The creature of a sage—it cannot be:
How could an aged anchoret,† grown old

* He is always called a Rajarshi, Rájá Rishi or Royal Saint. In the classification of sages there are three orders, the Rajarshi, or kingly sage, such as JANAKA, the Brahmarshi or Brahman sage as VASISHTHA, and the *Devarshi* or Divine Sage as NAREDA.

† *Nara* and *Náráyana* were two Saints, the sons of *Dherma* and *Ahinsá:* they devoted themselves to ascetic exercises which alarmed the Gods, and INDRA sent *Káma* and *Vasanta* or Love and Spring with the nymphs of heaven to inflame the sages with passion and thus end their penance. *Náráyana* observing the gambols of the party suspected their purpose—he invited them to approach, and treated them with so much civility, that they thought their object was attained. The sage, however, taking up a flower stalk, placed it on his thigh, when a beautiful nymph appeared, the superiority of whose charms covered the nymphs of heaven with shame. *Náráyana* then told them to return to *Indra*, and bear him a proof he needed not the company of beauty, in the present he made him of the new born nymph, who accompanied the Apsarases to Swerga, and was called *Urvási* from Uru a thigh. *Vámana Purána.* The Commentator on the drama says, *Nara* and *Náráyana* were *Avataras*, descents or incarnations of *Arjuna* and *Krishna.*

In dull devotion, and whose only merit
Was cold insensibility, conceive
Such supernatural beauty—oh no ; Love
Himself was her creator, whilst the Moon
Gave her his radiance, and the flowery Spring,
Taught her to madden men and gods with passion.

Urv. Where are our friends.

Chitr. The King will lead us to them.

Pur. Trust me they mourn your loss, nor is it strange
That they should miss your presence, when the eye
That once has viewed you—must lament your absence.

Urv. (*Apart.*) Delightful words, they fall like drops of [Nectar.
(*Aloud*) Not less my eagerness to see again
The friends I love.

Pur. Behold them there—they keep
Their anxious watch on *Hémakúta's* brow,
And mark your coming—safe from the Demon's grasp,
Like the bright moon emerging from eclipse.

Chitr. Look friend.

Urv. Like feelings fill my eyes as—

Chitr. Whose?

Urv. My friends.

Rembhá. Attended by each brilliant star.
Like *Chandra** in his radiant car,
The king appears and with him borne
Behold our sister nymphs return.

Menaká. For both the boons our thanks be poured ;
The prince unharmed and friends restored.

* Like the moon with the two stars of *Visákhá*, one of the lunar asterisms containing two stars.

Chorus. Joy to the prince who mighty rose
To quell the pride of demon foes.

Pur. To yonder lofty mountain guide the car.
(Apart.) Not vain our journey hitherward: 'tis much
In the unsteady rolling of the chariot
But for a moment to have touched the form
Of this celestial nymph—the blissful contact
Shoots extasy through every fibre. Here *(aloud.)*
Arrest our course—the maid's companion choir
Press on to her embrace, like flowery vines
That bend to catch the beauty of the spring.

Chorus. Joy to the king—Propitious Heaven
Has victory to his prowess given.

Pur. Behold in these my triumph.
(presenting Urvasi and Chitralekhá.)

Urv. My dear, dear Sisters, little did I hope
But late to feel once more this loved embrace.
(embraces them.)

Chorus. May countless ages blest survey
The mighty *Purúrava's* sway. *(a noise without.)*

Charioteer. (To the King.)
Sire from the east the rushing sound is heard
Of mighty chariots; yonder like clouds they roll
Along the mountain cliffs; now there alights
A chief in gorgeous raiment—like the blaze
Of lightening playing on the towering precipice.

Nymphs. Our king, great *Chitraratha.*

ENTER *Chitraratha, the king of the Gandharbas.**
(attended.)

Chitr. Illustrious victor, friend of *Indra* hail.

* The Gandharbas are the male attendants and Choristers in the Courts of Siva, Indra, and Kuvera.

Pur. King of the heavenly quiristers receive
The welcome of a friend*—What brings you hither.

Chitr. When *Indra* learnt from *Náreda* the rape
Of this fair damsel by the *Daitya, Kesi,*
He bade me gather the *Gandharba* train
And hasten to her rescue—I obeyed;
But ere we marched, news of your triumph came
And stopped our progress. For your friendly aid
I bear you now our monarch's thanks, and more—
His wish to see you in the heavenly courts,
Your worth has opened to your welcome visit—
This service is most dear to him—the nymph
Is now your boon—first given by *Náráyana*
To grace the halls of *Swerga*—now redeemed
From hands profane by your resistless valour.

Pur. You rate the deed too high; not mine the glory;
But his, the Thunderer's, from whom derived
The strength of those who conquer in his cause.
The very Echo of the Lion's roar,
As through the rocky rifts it spreads and deepens,
Appalls the mighty elephant.

Chitr. 'Tis well.
This modesty becomes your worth—Humility
Is ever found the ornament of valour.

Pur. Excuse me to the monarch—Other claims
Demand my distant presence; lead the nymph
Back to the king.

Chitr. Your will shall be obeyed.

Urv. (*Apart to Chitralekhá.*)
Speak for me my dear friend, my lips refuse
To bid adieu to my protector—Speak.

* The stage direction here is They shake hands. "Parasparam hastaw sprisatah"

Chitr. (*To the king*)

Illustrious Sir, my friend commands me ask
Your leave to carry back with her to heaven,
As one she dearly cherishes, your fame.

Pur. Farewell—I trust ere long to meet again.

The Gandharbas and Apsarasas ascend, Urvasí loiters and pretends to be stopped.

Urv. A moment pause. (*to Chitrálekhá.*) Dear Girl this straggling vine.
Has caught my garland—help me to get loose.

Chitr. No easy task I fear—you seem entangled
Too fast to be set free—but come what may
Depend upon my friendship.

Urv. Thanks, thanks,
Be mindful of your promise.

(*Chitralékhá employed in disengaging her*).

Pur. A thousand thanks, dear Plant, to whose kind aid
I owe another instant, and behold,
But for a moment and imperfectly,
Those half-averted charms.

Charioteer. Come Royal Sir,
Let us depart—the demon foes are hurled
Deep in the ocean wave—just punishment
For their rebellion against *Swerga's* king—
Now let the shaft, whose headlong force resembles
The blast of fate, sleep in its wonted quiver,
As cowers the snake within his gloomy covert.

(*They mount.*)

Pur. Ascend the car—

Urv. Ah! me—ah! when again
Shall I behold my brave deliverer.

(*Departs with Chitralékhá and the nymphs.*)

Puru. (*Looking after her.*)

What idle dreams does frantic love suggest;
What arduous tasks inspire—the beauteous nymph
Bears off my heart in triumph through the path
Her sire immortal treads: so flies the swan
Through the mid air, charged with its precious spoil,
The milky nectar of the Lotus stem.

(*Exit in his Car.*)

END OF THE FIRST ACT.

ACT II.

THE GARDEN OF THE PALACE OF PURURAVAS AT PRAYAGA.* (*Allahabad,*)

ENTER *Mánava, the Vidúshaka.*

It is mighty inconvenient this, for a Brahman like myself, one so much sought after and subject to such frequent invitation, to be burthened with the king's secret—going so much into company as I do, I shall never be able to set a guard upon my tongue. I must be prudent, and will stay here by myself in this retired temple, until my royal friend comes forth from the Council Chamber. (*Sits down and covers his face with his hands.*)

* It is also in other places called Pratisthána and is described as at the confluence of the Yamuná and Ganges on the bank of the latter: it should seem therefore that so late as the composition of this drama the ancient city still stood opposite to its present site—The ruins according to Hamilton are still to be seen at Jhusi on the left bank of the Ganges. *Hamilton's Genealogies of the Hindus.* Allahabad or Prayaga was a holy place having been the seat of *Bharadhwaja's* hermitage, but it never was a city until Akber made it one.

ENTER *Nipuniká, an Attendant on the Queen.*

The daughter of the king of *Kási** is quite sure that since the king returned from the regions of the sun, he is no longer the same—he must have left his heart behind him—what else can be the reason. I must try and find it out—if that crafty Brahman be in the secret I shall easily get at it. A secret can rest no longer in his breast, than morning dew upon thin grass—where can he be——eh——yes, there he sits—immoveable—like a monkey in a picture.—now to attack him, that is all I have to do. †*Arya—Mánava*—I salute you.

Man. Prosperity attend you. (*apart*). That sly baggage *Nipuniká*—she seeks to discover the secret I dare say. If so, she will get it to a certainty in spite of me, (*aloud*) Well *Nipuniká*, how is it you leave your music practice‡ for the garden.

Nip. The Queen has sent me to pay you a visit Sir.

Man. And what may be her Majesty's commands.

Nip. She bids me say that she has ever esteemed you as her good friend, and that it is therefore with some surprise she finds you utterly indifferent to her present anxiety.

Man. Why, what's the matter—you cannot suspect that my royal friend regards her grace with any diminution of his affection for her?

Nip. Oh! that is not the point—my mistress knows the cause of his melancholy well enough; nay more, he let out the secret himself, and in a fit of absence, addressed the Queen by the very name of his new love.

* The ancient name of Benares which is recognisable in the Cassidia of Ptolemy.

† A term of respect.

‡ *Sangida Bápára* for Sangita Vyápára. Practice of music, singing and dancing.

Man. (*Apart.*) Indeed—oh, if his majesty cannot keep his own secrets, why should I be plagued with them. (*aloud.*) Why what the deuce *Nipuniká*, did he call the Queen, *Urvasí*.

Nip. And pray who is *Urvasí*.

Man. The nymph—the *Apsaras*, ever since the king saw her, he has been out of his senses, he not only neglects her grace, but turns his back upon me.

Nip. (*Apart.*) So, so, I have settled that matter, as I expected. (*Aloud.*) Well I must return to the queen, what am I to say to her.

Man. Tell her I am weary of attempting to cure my friend the king, of this idle fancy of his. The only remedy, is the sight of her lotus countenance.

Nip. You may depend upon me. [*Exit.*

The Warder. (*without.*)

All hail to the monarch who toils through the day—
To shed o'er his subjects the light of his sway,
As travels unceasing the sun in his sphere
To chase from the universe darkness and fear—
The Lord of lone splendour an instant suspends
His course at mid-noon ere he westward descends,
And brief are the moments our young monarch knows,
Devoted to pleasure or paid to repose.*

* Frequent occasion will occur to notice the *Vaitálika*, a sort of poetical warder or Bard, who announces fixed periods of the day, as dawn and evening &c. in measured lines, and occasionally pours forth strains arising from any incidental occurrence—he here announces the arrival of the 6th hour or watch of the day, about two or three o'clock, in which alone he says the king can follow his own inclination.' It appears indeed that the royal station was by no means a sinecure: the Agni Purána lays down rules for the apportioning of the regal day,

Man. (*Listening*) Ha! my royal friend has risen from his seat, and is coming hither; I will await him.

but the same are more fully detailed in the last story of the Dasa Kumára, upon the authority of Chánakya, the celebrated minister of Chandragupta, who is always cited as the author of the *Niti*, or Institutes of Government. From the Dasa Kumára it appears that the day and night, was each divided into eight portions, corresponding accordingly to one hour and a half, and they are thus disposed of. Day—First portion. The king being dressed is to audit his accounts. Second—he is to pronounce judgment in suits appealed to him. Third—he is to breakfast. Fourth—he is to receive and make presents. Fifth to discuss political questions with his ministers and councillors. Sixth—he is, as stated in the drama, his own master. Seventh—he is to review the Troops. Eighth—he holds a military Council. Night. First portion. The king is to receive the reports of his spies and envoys. Second—he sups or dines. Third—he retires to rest after the perusal of some sacred work. The fourth and fifth portions or three hours are allowed for sleep. In the Sixth—he must rise and purify himself. In the Seventh, he holds a private consultation with his ministers and furnishes the Officers of Government with instructions, and the Eighth, is appropriated to the Purohit or Priest, the Brahman and religious ceremonies, after which the business of the day is resumed. The author of the play has conformed to this distribution—bringing Pururavas from Council at the sixth portion of the day—the precise hour depends upon the period of the year, the different portions being reckoned from sunrise, we may infer that the Poet intends this to be about 2 A. M. as at the end of the Act he makes the king describe the time as being past noon, when the heat is most oppressive—the Sixth watch accordingly begins in the drama about one o'clock.

ENTER *Purúravas.*

Pur. One glance sufficed ; the unerring shaft of love,
Laid bare the path, and gave a ready access
To that celestial nymph, to seat herself
Throned in my heart.

Man. (*To himself.*) Ah, that is exactly what the poor daughter of *Kásirája* complains of.

Pur. (*To the Vidúshaka.*) You have kept my secret safe.

Man. (*Apart.*) That baggage must have betrayed me, why else should he ask the question.

Pur. (*Alarmed.*) How, you are silent?

Man. Don't be alarmed—the fact is, that my tongue is so accustomed to the restraint I have put upon it, that I cannot answer off hand, even your enquiries.

Pur. 'Tis well—now then for recreation—
What shall we do?

Man. Pay a visit to the kitchen.

Pur. With what intent?

Man. Why the very sight of the savoury dishes in course of preparation will be sufficient to dissipate all melancholy ideas.

Pur. With you it may—for what you covet there
You may obtain—what my desires affect
Is hopeless—where should I then seek diversion.

Man. May I ask if the person of your highness was not beheld by the lady *Urvasí.*

Pur. What then.

Man. Why then I should think her not quite so uncomeatable.

Pur. Weigh it not thus, but judge impartially.

Man. What you say only adds to my surprise: what signifies madam *Urvasí's* unrivalled beauty, am I not equally without a peer, in ugliness.

Pur. Words cannot paint her every excellence.
Hear her *Mánavaka* described in brief.

Man. I am all attention.

Pur. Her loveliness yields splendour to her ornaments,
Her purity gives fragrance to her perfumes,
All the similitudes that poets use—
To picture beauty—it were gross flattery
To them, to name with her surpassing charms.

Man. This is mighty well, but in the fancy for such superhuman excellence, I should think your majesty had taken the *Chátaka** for your model; where please you shall we go.

Pur. To melancholy moods the only solace.
Is solitude—go onwards to the grove.

Man. (*Apart.*) What absurdity. (*Aloud.*) This way Sir, here is the boundary of the grove, and the southern wind† advances with due civility to meet you.

Pur. He comes to teach me, as he amorous sports
Amongst the blossoms of the *Mádhavi*‡
And dances frolic with the *Kunda*|| flowers,
With all the impassioned fervour of desire
And graceful ingenuity of love—
I mark in him my pictured sentiments.

Man. The only likeness I see is your mutual perseverance, but here we are, please you to enter.

* A Bird, said to drink no water but rain.

† During the hot weather the prevailing Breeze in Hindustan is from the South.

‡ A creeper with white flowers.

|| A kind of Jasmin.

Pur. Precede. I fear my coming hither vain,
Nor yield these shades relief to my affection—
Though with intent to gain tranquillity
I seek these paths of solitude and peace;
I feel like one contending with the stream
And still borne backwards by the current's force.

Man. Why entertain such feelings.

Pur. How avoid them.
What I affect is of no light attainment:
The very thought presumption—and now Love
The five armed God,* whose shafts already pierce me,
Calls to his aid these passion-breathing blossoms,
The mango's fragrant flowers and pallid leaves,
Light wafted round us by the southern breeze.

Man. Away with despondence, be assured that with a little coaxing, *Ananga*† will be your friend.

Pur. I take your words as ominous.

Man. But now let your highness notice the beauty of this garden, heralding as it were the presence of the spring.

Pur. I mark it well—In the *Kurúvaka,*
Behold the painted fingers of the fair
Red tinted in the midst and edged with ebony;
Here the *Asoka* puts forth nascent buds
Just bursting into flowers, and here the tendril
Round the brown mango's thickly clustering blossoms
To steal their fragrance, twines; methinks I see

* The Hindoo Cupid is armed with a bow strung with Bees and five arrows, each tipped with a flower and exercising peculiar influence on the heart.

† Love — the unembodied Deity. Having been once destroyed by *Siva*, burnt to ashes by the fire of his eye in resentment of *Káma's* aiming his darts at him.

The pride of spring on either hand attended
By budding infancy and flowering youth.

Man. The bower of Jasmines yonder is studded thick with blossoms, and the bees crowd about them in heaps; it invites your majesty to repose. (*They enter the Arbour.*)

Pur. As you please.

Man. Now seated in this shade you may dissipate your cares, by contemplating the elegant plants around us.

Pur. How should I learn composure—As my eye
Rests on the towering trees, and from their tops
Sees the lithe creeper wave, I call to mind
The graces that surpass its pendulous elegance.
Come, rouse your wit and friendship may inspire
Some capable expedient to secure me
The object of my wishes.

Man. With all my heart. The thunderbolt was *Indra's* friend, when he was in love with *Ahalyá** and I am your adviser now you are enamoured of *Urvasi.* We are both of us sapient councillors.†

Pur. Genuine affection ever councils wisely.

Man. Well I will turn the matter over in my mind, but you must not disturb my cogitations by your sighs.

Pur. (*Feeling his eyes twinkle.*)

* The wife of the sage Gautama—Indra enjoyed her by the contrivance Jupiter practised to possess Alcmena, the assumption of her husband's person, for which both were cursed by the sage. *Ahalyá* in consequence became a statue and was restored to animation only by the presence of Ramachandra.

† The insanity of both is alike, is the literal purport of the Vidúshakas remarks: if it were not for the Raja's reply this would seem applicable to the advised rather than the advisers.

The moon-faced maid is far beyond my reach!
Then why should love impart such flattering tokens,
They teach my mind to feel as if enjoyed
The present bliss, hope scarcely dares imagine.

(*They retire.*)

ENTER *Urvasí and Chitralékhá in the air.*

Chitr. Tell me dear girl your purpose: whither go we.

Urv. Nay, tell me first do you recall the promise
You made me jestingly upon the brow
Of *Hemakúta,* when your friendly hand
Detached my vesture from entangling thorns—
If it be still within your recollection
You need not ask me whither we proceed.

Chitr. You seek the moon of monarchs, *Purúravas.*

Urv. Right girl, though ill it argue of my modesty.

Chitr. Whom have you sent the envoy of your coming.

Urv. None, but my heart; that, has long gone before me.

Chitr. And who suggested such a tender visit.

Urv. 'Twas enjoined by love.

Chitr. I make no further question.

Urv. Aid me with your council, which way best
We may proceed, to meet with no impediment.

Chitr. There is no fear, the all-wise preceptor*
Of the immortals has imparted to you
The spell that renders you invincible
And mightier than the mightiest foe of heaven.†

* Vrihaspati, the planet Jupiter and teacher of the Gods.

† The meaning of the first part is perhaps not quite correct as the phrase is very doubtful, Aparájidam, nama, Sinha bandhana, vijjam. Aparájita náma Sikhá bandhana Vidyá. The unsurpassed crest-binding Science.

Urv. But you recall your promise.

Chitr. 'Tis retained
Firm in my heart—Behold where meet the streams
Of *Gangá* and of *Yamuna*—in the mirror
Of the broad waves, the palace of the king,
The crest borne gem of *Pratishthána,* views,
Complacently its own reflected glory.

Urv. The scene in truth might tempt us to believe
The fields of heaven were here in prospect spread—
But where to find its Lord, the pitying friend
Of all the helpless children of misfortune.

Chitr. Let us alight and hide us in this garden,
Whose groves may vie with *Indra's,* till we learn
Some news of him we seek.
Yonder I view him. (*They descend.*)
He waits thy coming to display his beauty
With undiminished brightness, like the moon,
That newly risen expects awhile his bride
The soft moon light, ere he put forth his radiance.

Urv. More graceful seems he than when first he met
My gaze.

Chitr. No doubt, come let us approch.

Urv. No, hold a moment—let us conceal ourselves
In veiling mist,* and lurking thus unseen

* Being visible to the audience and invisible to individuals on the stage is a contrivance familiar to the plays of various people, especially our own, as the Ghost of Hamlet, that of Banquo, Ariel in the Tempest, and Angelo in the Virgin Martyr, who repeatedly enters invisible; the wardrobe of some of our old Comedians comprised a robe to walk invisible, which Gifford supposes was a dress of light gauzy texture.

About the arbour, we may overhear
What thoughts—he utters in this solitude.
Communing with one only friend.

(They become invisible to the king and the Vidúshaka.)

Man. I have it, difficult as it is, I have hit upon a plan for securing you an interview with your Charmer.

Urv. (*Behind.*) How, who; what female is so blest to be
The object of his anxious thoughts.

Chitr. Be sure
It is no nymph of merely mortal origin.

Urv. Such lofty excellence fills me with fear.

Man. Did your Majesty hear me observe I had devised an expedient.

Pur. Say on, what is it.

Man. This it is—Let your Majesty cherish a comfortable nap, your union will then be effected by your dreams; or delineate a portrait of the Lady *Urvasí* and recreate your imagination by gazing on her picture.

Urv. Is then his heart indeed my own.

Pur. I fear me both impracticable.
How can I hope to taste repose that dreams
Might give me *Urvasí*, while fierce the shaft
Of *Káma** rankles in my breast; and vain,
The task her blooming graces to pourtray;
The tears of hopeless love at every line
Would fill my eyes, and hide her beauties from me.

Chitr. You hear.

Urv. I do, yet scarcely yet confide.

Something of the kind is used here apparently as the stage directions are 'covered with a veil, and "throwing aside the veil."

* The Hindu Cupid.

Man. Ah well, my ingenuity extends no farther.

Pur. Cold and relentless—little does she know,
Or knowing little heeds, my fond despair.
Yet cannot I reproach the archer God,
Although by giving to my hopes such aim,
He tortures me with barren, wild, desires.

Chirt. What say you now.

Urv. I grieve that he should deem me
Cold and unfeeling—I cannot now appear
Before I make these charges some reply:
Here is a *Bhúrja* leaf,* I will inscribe
My thoughts on it—and cast it in his way.

(She writes upon the leaf and lets it fall near the Vidushaka who picks it up.)

Man. Hola, what is here, the slough of a Snake dropped upon me.

Pur. It is a leaf and something written on it.

Man. No doubt the lady *Urvasí* unperceived, has over heard your lamentations, and sends this billet to console you.

Pur. Hope dawns upon my passion. *(Reads the leaf.)* Your guess was right.

Man. Oblige me then by letting me hear what is written.

Urv. Indeed, Sir, you are curious.

Pur. *(Reads.)*
" Not undeserved, although unknown, the flame.
" That glows with equal fires in either frame.
" The breeze that softly floats through heavenly bowers,
" Reclined upon my couch of coral flowers,

* A kind of Birch, the leaf of which is used as paper in some parts of Upper India, as that of the Palm is in the Peninsula.

"Sheds not on me its cool reviving breath
"But blows the hot and scorching gate of death:
"O'er all my form the fevered venom flies,
"And each bright bud beneath me, droops and dies"

Man. I hope you are pleased—you have now as much cause for rapture as I should consider it, to be civilly asked to dinner when I felt hungry.

Pur. How say you; cause for rapture—this dear leaf
Conveys indeed assurance most delightful:
Yet still I sigh to interchange our thoughts,
Met face to face, and eye encountering eye.

Urv. Our sentiments accord.

Pur. The drops that steal
Fast from my tremulous fingers may efface,
These characters traced by her tender hand:
Take you the leaf, and as a sacred trust
With care preserve it.

Man. Phoo, what matters it now—is it not enough that by the assenting sentiments of the lady *Urvasí*, your desire has borne flowers and promises fruit.

Urv. Now *Chitralekhá*, whilst I summon courage
To issue into view, do you appear,
And give the monarch notice of my purpose.

Chitr. I shall obey. *(Becomes visible.)* Hail to the king.

Pur. Fair damsel you are welcome; yet forgive me,
The less, your lovely friend comes not along:
The sacred streams before us shew less stately
Until they flow in unison.

Chitr. Royal Sir,
The cloud precedes the lightning.

Pur. Where is *Urvasí*:

You are inseparable.

Chitr. She salutes the king
And makes this her request.

Pur. Say, her command.

Chitr. Once by the enemy of the Gods assailed
And captive made, your valiant arm redeemed her.
Again in peril, she applies to you
And claims your guardian shield against a foe
More formidable still—from *Madana**
Whom you have armed against her.

Pur. You tell me gentle nymph your fair friend pines
With amorous passion—could you view my heart
You would be satisfied that love inflicts
Like anguish there—the God cements our souls
With mutual fervours—as in one mass combines
†Iron with iron when each fiery bar
With equal radiance glows.

Chitr. Appear, my friend—
The potent deity with like relentlessness
Afflicts the prince—and now to you I call
The herald of his sufferings.

Urv. *(appearing)* Faithless friend
Thus to desert me.

Chitr. It will soon be seen
Which merits best the title of deserter
Mean while, think where you are.

Urv. Triumph to the king.

Pur. The wish is victory,

* Another name of *Kama* or Cupid.

† The art of welding Iron was therefore known to the Hindus.

When from the Sovereign of the Gods transferred
By lips celestial to a mortal monarch.*
(Take her hand and leads her to a seat.)

Man. Fair Lady I am the Brahman of the King, and his friend, and so may claim some notice (*Urvasi bows to him smiling.*) Prosperity attend you.

A Messenger of the Gods in the air.

Mess. Ho—*Chitralekha*—*Urvasi* repair
Swift to the palace of the Lord of air;
There your appointed duties to fulfill
And give expression to the wondrous skill—
Of *Bharata* your master†—to the dome
Divine, the world's protecting rulers‡ come,

* That is, the customary wish with which *Indra* is addressed when applied by you to a mortal is in fact a boon to that effect. The words are *Jayadu Jayadu Mahárao*—May the great prince conquer.

† *Bharata* is the supposed inventor of dramatic composition.

‡ The *Lokapálas* or Guardians of the world are sometimes confounded with the deities presiding over the different cardinal points, but this is not quite correct, and they are more properly the divinities who were appointed by *Brahmá* upon the creation of the world, to act as rulers over the different kinds of created things: the list occurs in several Puranas—but the following is from the *Mahabharat*, the *Harivansa* portion.

Indra, Sovereign of the three *Lokas*, or Earth and the Regions above and below.

Soma—Of Sacrifices, ascetic rites, the lunar and solar asterisms, Brahmans and healing herbs.

Daksha—Of the *Prajápatis* the patriarchs or first created and progenitors of mankind.

Varuna—Of the Waters.

Vaiswánara—Of the *Pitris* or Manes.

Váyu—Of the *Gandherbas*, of unembodied element, of time and sound.

Eager to view the scene that genius fires
That passion animates, and truth inspires.

Chitr. Hear you my friend, be speedy in your parting.

Urv. I cannot speak.

Mahádeva—Of the *Mátris*, of the spirits of ill, of kine, of portents and planets, of infirmities and diseases, and of Ghosts.

Vaisravana—Of the *Yakshas*, *Rakshasas*, *Guhyakas*, of wealth and of all precious gems.

Sesha—Of the entire Serpent race.

Vásuki—Of the *Nágas* or Ophite tribes of *Pátála*.

Takshaka—younger brother of the *Adityas*. Of Snakes.

Parjánya—Of Oceans, rivers, clouds, and rain.

Chitraratha—Of the *Gandherbas*.

Kámadeva—Of the *Apsarases*.

Nandi the bull of *Síva*, of all quadrupeds.

Hiranyáksha and *Hiranyákasipu*, of the *Daityas*.

Viprachitti—Of the *Dánavas*.

Mahákála—Of the *Ganas* or *Siva's* attendants.

Vritra—Of the children of *Anáyusha* the wife of *Twashtri*.

Ráhu the son of *Sinhiká*—Of evil portents and prodigies.

Samvatsara—Of the divisions of time from the twinkling of an eye to the period of an age.

Superna—Of Birds of prey.

Garura—Of the winged race.

Aruna—the brother of *Garura* was made by *Indra*, ruler in the East.

Yama the son of *Aditya* in the South.

The son of *Kasyapa*, *Amburaja*, in the West.

Pingala the son of *Pulastya* in the North.

Having thus nominated the Presiding Spirits, various *Lokas* or districts were created by *Swayambhu*—as brilliant as the sun or fire, radiant as lightning, or chastely beaming as the Moon, of various colours, moveable at will, many hundreds of *Yojanas* in extent, the fit abodes of the pious, exempt from sin and pain. Those Brahmans whose merit shines conspicuous are elevated to these regions, those who practice piety and worship devoutly, who are upright and benevolent, free from cupidity and cherishers of the poor.

Having thus distributed his

Chitr. Forgive us mighty Prince:
We have our stated tasks, and must obey—
Not yours the wish we wanton should provoke
The dread displeasure of the king of heaven.

Pur. You judge me right; not mine the impious thought
But for an instant to withhold obedience
To his high will—Farewell—but let me ever
Live in your memory.

(Urvasi and Chitralekhá depart.)

Pur. *(To the Vidúshaka.)* She disappears: What else deserves my gaze.

sons, *Brahma* departed to his own dwelling *Pushkara*. The Deities rambled through the districts, and engaged in the charges respectively assigned them, being all cherished by *Mahendra*. The Gods, with *Indra* at their head, as placed by *Swayambhu* discharging their guardian duties obtained fame and heaven, and receiving their share of sacrifices enjoyed prosperity and happiness.

Some of the early sections of the *Kási k'hand* of the *Skánda Purana* or from the 9th to the 23d contain a description of the several *Lokas*, the cities or spheres of the different divinities as they are traversed by *Sivasermá* on his way from earth to the region of Siva— He passes in this route the *Lokas* of the nymphs, of the Sun, of *Indra*, *Agni*, *Nirrhita*, *Varuna*, *Váyu*, *Kuvera*, of the *Ganas* or attendants of *Siva*, of *Soma*, of the lunar asterisms, of *Budha* *Sukra*, *Bhauma*, *Guru* and *Sani* or the planets Mercury, Venus, Mars, Jupiter and Saturn, of the seven *Rishis*, of *Dhruva*, the *Lokas* called *Maharloka*, *Janaloka* and *Tapoloka*, and that called *Satyaloka*, the abode of *Brahma*, and *Vaikuntha* and *Kailas* or the regions severally of *Vishnu* and *Siva*. This disposition of the spheres however has evidently received a peculiar colouring from the Pauranic Cosmography, and the sectarial bias of the *Skánda Purána*.

Man. Why perhaps this—*(looking for the Bhúrja leaf.* *(apart.)* Bless me, I have been so fascinated myself by the smiles of the lady *Urvasi,* that the leaf with her billet upon it, has unconsciously slipped out of my hands.

Pur. You were about to speak.

Man. Yes, I was going to say—do not lose your fortitude—you are firmly attached to the nymph, and depend on it she is just as fervently devoted to you.

Pur. Of that I feel assured: the sighs that heaved
Her panting bosom as she hence departed
Exhaled her heart, and lodged it in my bosom,
Free to dispose of it, although her person
Be forced to wait upon a master's will*

Man. (apart.) I am all in a flutter lest he should ask me for that abominable leaf.

Pur. What shall console my eyes—give me the leaf.

Man. The leaf, dear me, it is not here—it must have gone after *Urvasi.*

Pur. How could you be so heedless ; search about.

They search for the leaf and retire.

ENTER *in the foreground, Ausinari, the Queen, with Nipuniká and attendants.*

Ausi. You saw his highness you are sure *Nipuniká,*

Nip. Why should your majesty doubt my report.

Ausi. Well, let us seek him then, and unobserved.
Amidst these shades we may detect the truth.

* Rowe is less daring, altho' in the Rival Queens he makes Alexander say something of this kind.

Alex. (*To Statira*) My fluttering heart tumultuous with its bliss.
Would leap into thy bosom-

But what is yon that meets us like a shred
Of some rent garment, floating on the wind.

Nip. A *Bhojpatr* leaf—there seem to be some marks like letters upon it; it is caught by your grace's anclet. (*Picks it up.*) Will it please you read it.

Ausi. Glance o'er its tenor, and if not unfit
To meet our ear—peruse what there is written.

Nip. It looks like a memorial verse: eh, no; now it strikes me—they must be lines addressed by *Urvasi* to the king; this is some carelessness now of that blockhead *Mánavaka.*

Ausi. Read, I shall conceive its purport.

Nip. (*Reads the lines as above.*)

Ausi. Enough, proceed, and with this evidence,
We shall confound our nymph-enamoured swain.

They go round the arbour, the King and Mánavaka advance.

Man. Eh, is not that the leaf yonder on the mount just on the edge of the garden.

Pur. Breeze of the south, the friend of love and spring,
Though from the flower you steal the fragrant down
To scatter perfume—yet why plunder me
Of those dear characters, her own fair hand
In proof of her affection traced—thou knowest
The lonely lover that in absence pines
Lives on such fond memorials—It is not
Thy wont to disregard a lover's suit.

Man. No, I was mistaken, I was deceived by the tawny hue of the Peacock's tail.

Pur. I am every way unhappy.

Ausínarí and her train advance.

Ausi. Nay my good Lord
I pray you be consoled, if as I deem

The loss of this occasion your distress.

(*Offering the leaf.*)

Pur. (*Apart.*) The Queen. (*Aloud.*) Madam you are welcome.

Ausi. You do not think me so.

Pur. (*To the Vidúshaka apart.*) What is to be done.

Man. I dont know: what excuse can a free booter offer when he is taken in the fact.

Pur. This is no time to jest. (*Aloud.*) Believe me madam,
This leaf was not the object of my search,
Nor cause of my anxiety.

Ausi. Excuse me
If I suspect that your denial seeks
But to conceal the truth.

Man. Your grace had better order dinner—that will be the most effectual remedy for his majestys bile.

Ausi. You hear *Nipuniká* this most sage councillor,
And how he would remove his friend's distress.

Man. Why not Madam. Is not every body put into good humour by a hearty meal.

Pur. Peace Blockhead, you but heighten my offence.

Ausi. Not yours the offence my lord: 'tis mine, who tarry.
Here, where my presence is not wished, 'tis soon
Removed (*Going.*)

Pur. Yet stay—I owe myself to blame—
Curb your resentment—that alone convicts me:
When monarchs are incensed it cannot be
But that their slaves are guilty. (*falls at her feet.*)

Ausi. Think me not,
So mere a child—that this assumed respect
Beguiles me of my wrath—Away with it—

'Tis gross my lord, and sets but ill upon you.
I treat such hypocritical penitence
As it deserves. *(Spurns him and exit.)*

Man. Her majesty has gone off in a hurry like, a river in the rains—You may rise. (*To the king who has continued prostrate.*)

Pur. I might have spared myself the pains.
A woman is clear sighted—and mere words
Touch not her heart—Passion must give them credit.
The lapidary master of his craft
With cold indifference eyes the spurious gem.

Man. You care very little about this I suppose; the eye that is dazzled with light cannot bear the lamp.

Pur. Not so, 'tis true that *Urvasí* engrosses
My heart, but *Kásirája's* daughter claims
My deference—less indeed, that her contempt
Disdains my protestations—and this scorn
Will justify requital.

Man. Well, let us have done with her majesty—and think a little of a famished brahman: it is high time to bathe and eat.

Pur. 'Tis past mid-day—exhausted by the heat
The Peacock plunges in the scanty pool
That feeds the tall tree's root: the drowsy Bee
Sleeps in the hollow chamber of the Lotus
Darkened with closing petals—on the brink
Of the now tepid lake the wild Duck lurks
Amongst the sedgy shade; and even here—
The Parrot from his wiry bower complains
And calls for water to allay his thirst. [*Exeunt.*

END OF THE SECOND ACT.

ACT III.

SCENE I. THE HERMITAGE OF BHARATA.

ENTER ***Gálava and Pailava*† *two of his disciples.*

Gal. Well, friend *Pailava*—what news—whilst you were at *Makendra's* palace with the Sage, I have been obliged

* *Galava* was a saint of some note, and is the hero of a long legend in the *Udyoga Parva* of the *Mahábhárat*—He there appears as the pupil of *Viswamitra.* At the expiration of his studies he importuned his master so tell him what present he should make him—*Viswamitra* being out of humor at last desired him to bring him 800 horses, each of a white colour, with one black ear. *Gálava* in his distress applied to *Garura* who was his particular friend, and with him repaired to *Yayáti* king of *Pratishthána.* *Yayáti* being unable to comply with the sage's wish presented him his daughter *Mádhavi,* whom *Gálava* gave in marriage successively to *Haryaswa* king of *Ayodhyá, Divodása* king of *Kási, Usinara* king of *Bhoja,* and received from each upon the birth of a son by her, two hundred of the steeds he was in quest of. These horses were originally a thousand in number. The saint *Richika* having demanded the daughter of *Gádhi* sovereign of *Kanyakubja* as his wife, that prince to evade the match, being afraid to decline it, required the steeds in question as a present in return. *Richika* obtained them from the God of ocean, *Varuna,* and transferred them to his father in law by whose descendants 600 were sold to different princes, and the rest given away to the Brahmans. *Gálava* having procured the horses which were in possession of the kings took them and the Damsel, still by virtue of a boon a virgin, and presented them together to *Viswamitra.* The sage received them and begot a son by her, *Ashtaka,* to whom he resigned

ed to stay at home to look after the holy Fire—Were the Immortals pleased with the specimen of our master's skill.

Pail. How could they chuse but be pleased: there was eloquence and melody for them—the Drama was *Lakshmi's* choice of a Lord*—the nymph *Urvasí* quite lost herself in the impassioned passages.

Gal. There is something not quite right implied in your applause.

Pail. Very true, for unluckily *Urvasí* forgot her part.

Gal. How so?

Pail. You shall hear. *Urvasí*—played *Lakshmí, Menaká* was *Váruni*, the latter says—

> *Lakshmí* the mighty powers that rule the spheres
> Are all assembled: at their head appears,
> The blooming *Késava*: Confess—to whom
> Inclines your heart—

his hermitage, and his stud, and retired to the woods: the place was thence called *Ashtakapur.* The lady after this was reconducted by *Gálava* to her father, and he in imitation of his preceptor spent the rest of his days in solitary devotion.

† *Paila* is the name of a *Rishi*, by whom the *Rig Veda* was arranged, and sub-divided into two portions. It is not certain that he is intended in this place, by the name *Pailava* although not unlikely.

* Or the *Lakshmi Swayamvara*: it was common in the Hindu Society of former times for Princesses, and women of rank to select a husband for themselves. The candidates for the hand of the Lady were invited to her father's house, and after previous festivities for some days, were collected in a hall, round which the damsel passed and selected her future Lord, by throwing a garland round his neck: the marriage rite was then celebrated as usual: the custom is the subject of much pleasing poetic description, in the *Mahábhárat*, the *Naishadha* and other works: a translation of the *Swayamvara* of *Draupadi* from the former is published in the Calcutta Quarterly Magazine for Sept. 1825.

Her reply should have been—To *Puru-shottama;* but instead of that—To *Puru-rava,* escaped her lips.

Gal. The intellectual faculties are but the slaves of destiny—Was not the sage much displeased?

Pail. He immediately denounced a curse on her, but she found favour with *Mahendra.*

Gal. How so?

Pail. The sentence of the Sage was, that as she had forgotten her part, so should she be forgotten in heaven; but when the performance was over, *Indra* observing her as she stood apart, ashamed and disconsolate, called her o him, The mortal who engrossed her thoughts, he said, had been his friend in the hour of peril—he had aided him effectually in conflict with the enemies of the Gods, and was entitled to some acknowledgment—The anger of the Seer had banished her from heaven for a while—consequently she must depart his Court, but she might spend her term of exile with the Monarch: the period of her banishment is to expire when the king beholds the offspring she shall bear him.

Gal. This was like *Mahendra*—he knows all hearts.

Pail. Come, Come! we have been chattering here till it is almost the time when our Preceptor performs his ablutions. Come, we have no time to lose—let us attend him.

Exeunt.

SCENE II.

PART OF THE GARDENS OF THE PALACE.

ENTER *the Chamberlain.*

As long as life is vigorous a man endures labour for the sake of procuring ease—when further advanced in age, his toils are lightened by the participation of his children: but when he is old, he reaps nothing from his exertions, but fatigue—my strength is daily undermined and my body exhausted by this servitude—waiting on women is the devil—I am now to find the King, and tell him that her majesty having dismissed all anger and resentment, is desirous of paying her homage to him this evening, for the completion of the vow in which she has engaged.* The close of the day is agreeable enough here in the palace. The Peacocks nod upon their perches and the Doves flock to the turret tops—scarcely distingishable from the incense that flows through the lattices of the lofty chambers. Th venerable servants of the inner apartment are all busily engaged in propitiatory rites, and substituting lamps for the offerings of flowers that decorated the holy shrines throughout the day. Ah, here comes the prince, attended by the damsel train with flambeaux in their delicate hands: he moves like a mountain, around whose stately skirts, the slender *Karnikára* spreads its brilliant blossoms. I will wait him here.

ENTER *Purúravas and the Vidúshaka with female attendants*† *carrying torches.*

So ends the day, the anxious cares of state
Have left no interval for private sorrow,

* Obligations self imposed are in constant practice amongst the Hindus. In this case the Queen has engagd to forego her ornaments and to hold a rigid fast untill the moon enters a certain asterism.

† This might be supposed a Copy of Mohammedan manners but it is not necessarily so, having been the practice of the Hindus before the Christian era for the king's person when within the palace used to be attended by women—his guards and other troops being stationed without the gates. Thus Strabo.

Regis corpus mulieres curant, ea quoque de parentibus emptæ, qui Regem custodiunt, et reliquus exercitus manent extra portas. IV. 15.

But how to pass the night : its deary length
Affords no promise of relief.

Chamberlain, (advances,) Glory to the king. So please your Grace, Her Majesty expresses a wish to be honoured with your presence on the terrace of the Pavilion of gems, to witness from it the entrance of the Moon into the asterism Rohini.

Pur. Go my good friend—apprise her majesty
She may dispose of us. [*Exit Chamberlain.*
What think you that the Queen
Proposes by the vow she has assumed.

Man. I suppose she repents of herpettishness, and wishes to be friends with you again: this is but an excuse to bring you to her presence when she may efface the recollection of the indignity with which she treated you.

Pur. 'Tis very likely—Prudent wives full soon
Repent the scorn that urged them to repel
An humbled husband, and are glad to seek
Some fair pretext to win his love again—
We will indulge her grace—On to the chamber.

Man. 'Tis here : ascend these steps of crystal, smooth shining as the waters of the Ganges—the Pavilion of gems is particularly lovely when evening sets in. *(they ascend.)* The moon is just about to rise—the east is tinged with red.

Pur. 'Tis even so : illumined by the rays
Of his yet unseen orb, the evening glooms
On either hand retire, and in the midst
The radiance spreads like a fair face that smiles
Betwixt the jetty curls on either brow
In clusters pendulous—I could gaze for ever.

Man. Ho, here he comes, the king of the Brahmans, as beautiful as a ball of Almonds and Sugar.

Pur. Oh base similitude—your thoughts my friend
Have rarely nobler prompter than your Stomach.

Carries his hands to his forehead and bows to the moon now risen.

Hail-glorious Lord of night whose tempered fires
Are gleaned from Solar fountains, but to yield
The virtuous, fruit eternal, as they light
The flame of holy sacrifice—whose stores
Ambrosial serve but to regale the Gods
And the immortal fathers of mankind—
All hail to thee—whose rising ray dispels
The glooms of eve, and whose pale crescent crowns
The glorious diadem of *Mahádeva.**

Man. Enough, Sir your grand father without whose assent we Brahmans can do nothing, bids you sit, that he may repose himself.

Puru. (*Makes the Vidúshaka sit and then seats himself.*)
The splendour of the Moon is light enough:
Remove the torches and command my train
Retire to rest.

* The first of these specifications refers to the astronomical facts of the moon's deriving its light from the sun, and by its positions forming the days of the lunar month, on which particular ceremonies are to be observed—in the latter case it is supposed to move in the *Mandala* the sphere or orbit of the sun, and when in conjunction as at the new moon or *Amávasya* funeral obsequies are especially to be celebrated. According to mythological notions also the moon is the grand receptacle and store house of *Amrit* or Ambrosia which it supplies during the fortnight of its wane to the Gods and on the last—day to the *Pitris* or deified progenitors. As personified, the moon is the father of *Budha* and grandfather of *Pururavas* as already shewn. The half moon, as frequently noticed, is worn by *Siva* upon his forehead.

Attendant. As you command (*withdraws with the torch bearers.*)

Puru. I think we may not yet expect the Queen :
And now we are alone I would impart
My thoughts.

Man. Out with them—there is no appearance of her yet, aud it is well to keep up your spirits with hope.

Puru. You council well—In truth my fond desire
Becomes more fervid as enjoyment seems
Remote, and fresh impediments obstruct
My happiness—like an impetuous torrent,
That checked by adverse rocks a while delays
Its course, till high with chafing waters swollen,
It rushes past with aggravated fury.

Man. There is one thing to be said: notwithstanding your anxiety has made you something thinner it has rather improved than impaired your personal appearance—I argue from this that a meeting with the nymph is not very distant.

Pur. My right arm by its glad pulsation soothes
My grief, like you with hope inspiring words.

Man. A Brahman's words be assured are never uttered in vain.

(ENTER *above in a heavenly car Urvasí and Chitralékhá Urvasí in a purple dress with pearl ornaments.**)

Urvasí. Now my dear Girl—
What say you—do these purple robes become me
Thus trimmed with pearls

* The text is *Abhisáriká Veshá*, the garb of a woman who goes to meet her lover—the Specification of the translation is from *Urvasi's* first speech —the term is *Nila* which means dark blue or black—most ordinarily the former..

Chitr. I cannot think of words
To speak my admiration—only this,
Would I were *Pururavas.*

Urva. My dear Friend
I feel my strength desert me; do you lead me
Quick to his Royal Palace.

Chitr. View it here,
White gleaming in the Moon-light, whilst below
The *Yamunás* blue waters wash its foot.
Like the Snow tufted summits of *Kailása*
Rising in radiance from their bosky base.
Advance.

Urva. One moment—exercise the power
Of meditative vision: where is the King
The master of my heart and what employs him.

Chitr (*apart.*) I will rouse her fears.
I see him—in a fit solitude he waits
Impatiently the coming of the bride
(*Urvasí expresses despair.*)
How, Silly wench—what else would you desire
Should be his occupation—

Urva. Ah my friend,
My flutterihg heart is easily alarmed.

Chitr. In the Pavilion of bright gems awaits
The king, his trusty friend alone attends him
Let us thither.

Urv. Proceed.

(*They descend and leave the car.*

Puru. As spreads the Moon its lustre, so my Love
Grows with advancing night.

Urv. Ah, me—I fear.

Even yet to trust—let us remain invisible
And overhear their conference till doubt
Be all dispersed.

Chitr. Be it as you will.

Man. The rays of the Moon are charged with Ambrosia—do you find no benefit from them.

Puru. Small is their power, or that of aught, to mitigate
The pangs of Love. Soft beds of fragrant flowers
Sandal's cool unguent, strings of gelid pearl,
And these mild tempered rays, exhaust on me
In vain their virtue—nothing can allay
The fever of my heart—She, she alone
The Goddess I adore, with a few words
Of magic potency can charm my woes
And yield me rest. This arm that pressed her side,
When through etherial fields we rapid drove,
Is warm with life, all else exanimate,
Cumbers the earth a dull and useless burthen

Urv. I need no more concealment *(She advances hastily)*
Woe is me;
He deigns not to regard me—

Chitr. In your haste
You have forgotten to put off the veil
That screens you from his sight.

Behind—This way your grace

(All listen—Urvasí throws herself into the arms of Chitralékhá)

Man. The Queen is here—we had better be mute.

Puru. Assume the semblance of indifference.

Urv. What shall we do?

Chitr. Remain invisible.

Urv. Not long her purposed stay: by her attire
She holds some sacred vow.

(Enter *the Queen with attendants bearing offerings, the Queen is dressed in white—flowers are her only ornaments.)*

Queen. This union with the constellation yields
New brilliance to the Lord of Rohini.*

Attendants. Such effect attends your grace's encounter with his Majesty.

Man. *(to Purúravas.)* She comes I imagine to offer her benedictions, or under the semblance of a solemn vow, she wishes to obliterate the recollection of the indignity with which she lately repelled your advances—Well, I think her majesty looks very charming to-day.

Puru. In truth she pleases me; thus chastely robed
In modest white—her clustering tresses decked
With sacred flowers alone†—her haughty mien
Exchanged for meek devotion—thus arrayed
She moves with heightened charms.

Queen. *(advancing)* Hail to the King.

Attendant. Hail to the King.

Puru. Madam you are welcome. *(leads her to a seat.)*

Urv. *(behind)* She merits to be called divine‡—the bride
Of Heaven's great King|| boasts not surpassing dignity.

Chitr. Your commendations speak you free from envy.

Queen. My gracious Lord, I have imposed on me
A voluntary vow, the term of which
Is nigh at hand—I would solicit you,
Bear with the inconvenience that my presence
May for brief time occasion you.

* The Moon.

† Or with the blossoms of the holy *Durva* Grass.

‡ *Devi*, or Goddess is one of the titles appropriate to the state of Queen.

|| *Sachi* the wife of *Indra*,

Puru. You do me wrong,
Your presence is a favour.

Man. May all the inconvenience light upon those who would disturb such interchange of good wishes.

Pur. *(To the Queen)* How call you your observance?

Nip. *(On the Queen's turning to her.)* The conciliation of regard*

Pur. Is it even so—yet trust me it is needless
To wear this tender form, as slight and delicate
As the lithe Lotus stem, with rude austerity.
In me behold your slave, whom to propitiate
Claims not your care, your favour is his happiness.

Urv. *(Smiling scornfully)* He pays her mighty deference.

Chitr. So he should—
When the heart strays, the tongue is most profuse
Of bland professions to the slighted wife.

Queen. Not vain my vow, since it already wins me
My lord's complacent speech.

Man. Enough said on both sides, these civilities require no further reply.

Queen. Come Girls, the offerings, that I may present them
To the bright Deity, whose rays diffuse
Intenser lustre on these splendid walls.

Attendant. Here are the perfumes Madam, here the flowers, *(gives them, and the Queen goes through the usual form of presenting the Arghya or oblation of fruits, perfumes, flowers, &c.)*

Queen. These cates present *Mánavaka,* and these
Give to the Chamberlain.

* *Piya passádana.*

(The Attendant takes a tray of Sweetmeats first to the Vidúshaka and then to the Kanchukí)

Man. Prosperity attend your highness, may your fasts ever end in a feast.

Chamberlain. Prosperity to the Queen.

Queen. Now with your grace's leave I pay you homage.

(Presents oblations to the King, bows and falls at his feet, then rises.)

Resplendent pair who o'er the night preside,
Lord of the Deer born* banneret and thou
His favourite, ROHINI†—hear and attest
The sacred promise that I make my husband.
Whatever nymph attract my Lord's regard,
And share with him the mutual bonds of love,
I henceforth treat with kindness and complacency.

* The car of the moon is decorated with a small flag on which a deer is represented.

* *Chandra* or the Moon is fabled to have been married to the twenty seven daughters of the Patriarch *Daksha*, or, *Aswini* and the rest, who are in fact personifications of the Lunar Asterisms. His favourite amongst them, was *Rohini*, to whom he so wholly devoted himself as to neglect the rest—they complained to their father, and *Daksha* repeatedly interposed, till finding his remonstrances vain he denounced a curse upon his son-in-law, in consequence of which he remained childless, and became affected by consumption. The wives of *Chandra* having interceded in his behalf with their father, *Daksha* modified an imprecation which he could not recall, and pronounced that the decay should be periodical only, not permanent, and that it should alternate with periods of recovery. Hence the successive wane and increase of the Moon. *Padma Purána, Swerga Khanda* Sec. II. *Rohini* in astronomy is the fourth Lunar Mansion, containing five stars, the principal of which is Aldebaran.

Urv. Oh my dear friend, how much these words assuage
The apprehensions of my heart.

Chitr. She is a Lady
Of an exalted spirit, and a wife
Of duty most exemplary—you now
May rest assured, nothing will more impede
Your union with your love.

Man. *(Apart to Purúravas.)* The culprit that is caught, and gets off with the loss of a hand instead of his life determines to reform. *(aloud)* Surely your grace cannot think his Majesty a person of such a disposition.

Queen It matters not. If my enjoyment cease,
I would not therefore that his grace should feel
The least restraint. I leave him to his liberty.
Think you, wiseSir, this license is unwelcome.

Pura.. I am not what you doubt me—but the power
Abides with you: do with me as you will—
Give me to whom you please, or if you please
Retain me still your slave.

Queen. Be what you list.
My vow is plighted—nor in vain the rite.
If it afford you satisfaction—come—
Hence, Girls—'tis time we take our leave.

Puru. Not so
So soon to leave me is no mark of favour.

Queen. You must excuse me—I may not forego
The duties I have solemnly incurred.

[*Exit with train.*

Urv. Why, Girl, I doubt the Raja still affects
His queen—so be it—it is now too late
For me to hope my heart can be reclaimed.

Chitr. Away with doubt, you have no need to fear.

Pur. Is the Queen far removed.

Man. You may say whatever you wish, safely enough: you are fairly given over by her, like a sick man by his physician.

Pur. I fear I am, by faithless *Urvasi.*

Would she were here—and that the gentle music
Of her rich Anklets murmured in my ears;
Or that her lotus hands, as with light step
She stole behind me, spread a tender veil
Before my eyes—that in this shady bower
She deigned descend spontaneous, or drawn hither
With welcome violence by some fair friend –
Ha, the lovely daughter of *Náráyana.*

(*Urvasi has advanced behind the king and covers his eyes with her hands.*)

Vid. How knows your grace.

Pur. It must be *Urvasi*—

No other hand could shoot such extasy
Through this emaciate frame: the Solar ray
Wakes not the night's fair blossom—that alone,
Expands when conscious of the moon's dear presence.

Urv. (*Appearing,*) Joy to the king.

Pur. All hail bright nymph of heaven.

(*Leads her to a seat*)

Chitr. (*Advancing.*) Be the king blest.

Pur. I feel I am already.

Urv. Hear me my friend. (*To Chitralekhá*)

By virtue of the gift
Made of his royal person by the Queen,
I boldly claim the king. Do you declare,

If I am reprehensible.

Man. What were you here ever since Sunset.

Pur. I have no purpose to dispute the claim;
But let me ask, if such assent were needed,
Who was it that first granted you permission
To rob me of my heart.

Chitr. My friend, I know,
Can proffer no reply—then let this be.
Now grant me my request, I must depart
To minister to *Chandra* till the term
Of the Spring festival—till my return
Be careful that this nymph have never cause
To mourn the Heaven she has resigned for thee.

Man. Heaven indeed, why should she ever think of such a place—a place where they neither eat, not drink, nor close their eyes even for a twinkle.*

* The Gods are supposed to be exempt from the momentary elevation and depression of the upper Eyelid, to which mortals are subject, and to look with a firm unintermittent gaze. Hence a deity is termed *Animisha* and *Animesha*—one whose eyes do not twinkle. Various allusions to this attribute occur in Poetry. When *Indra* visits *Sita* to encourage her, he assumes at her request the marks of divinity—he treads the air, and suspends the motion of the eyelids. *Rámáyana.* When *Agni Varuna*, *Yama* and *Indra* all assume the form of *Nala* at the marriage of *Damayanti*, she distinguishes her mortal lover by the twinkling of his eyes, whilst the Gods are *Stabdha Lochana*, fixed-eyed. *Mahábhárat*, *Nalopákhyán*. And when the *Aswini Kumáras* practice the same trick upon the bride of *Chyavana*, she recognises her husband by this amongst other indications. *Padma Purána.* The notion is the more deserving of attention, as it is one of those coincidences with Classical Mythology which can scarcely be accidental. *Heliodorus* says "The Gods may be known by the eyes looking with a fixed

Pur. The heaven of *Indra* is the eternal source
Of joy ineffable: it cannot be,
The cares of *Purúravas* should efface
The memory of immortal bliss—
Yet, nymph, of this be confident, my soul
Shall know no other sovereign than your friend.

Chitr. 'Tis all I ask—be happy *Urvasi*
And bid me now adieu.

Urv. (*Embracing her.*) Forget me not.

Chitr. That, I should rather beg of you, thus blest
With one the only object of your wishes.

[*Bows to the king and Exit.*

Man. Fate is propitious and crowns your Majesty's desires.

Pur. 'Tis true, I reach the height of my ambition.
The haughty canopy that spreads it's shade
Of universal empire o'er the world;
The footstool of dominion set with gems
Torn from the glittering brows of prostrate kings,
Are in my mind less glorious than to lie
At *Urvasi's* fair feet, and do her bidding.

Urv. I have not words to speak my gratitude.

Pur. Now I behold thee thus, how changed is all
The current of my feelings—these mild rays
Cool, vivifying, gleam—the shafts of *Madana*

regard; and never closing the eyelids, and he cites Homer in proof of it. An instance from the Iliad which he has not noticed, may be cited perhaps as an additional confirmation, and the *marble eyes* of Venus by which Helen knew the Goddess, and which the commentators, and translators seem to be much perplexed with, are probably the *Stabdha lochana*, the fixed eyes of the Hindus—full, and unveiled even for an instant, like the eyes of a marble Statue.

Are now most welcome—all that was but late
Harsh and distasteful to me, now appears
Delightful by your presence.

Urv. I lament,
I caused my Lord to suffer pain so long.

Pur. Nay, say not so, the Joy that follows grief
Gains richer zest from agony foregone—
The traveller who faint pursues his track
In the fierce day, alone can tell how sweet,
The grateful shelter of the friendly tree.

Man. The moon is high—it were as well to go in.

Pur. Conduct the way—and dearest let me trust
The moon that smiles to night on our espousals,
Shall shine through many a happy year to come
Auspicious on our Union.*

[*Exeunt into the Pavilion.*

* The translation is not very close here, the deviation is partly intentional, partly unavoidable, as the manuscript of the original is incorrect and the Comment is silent.

END OF THE THIRD ACT.

ACT IV.*

SCENE. *The Forest of Akalusha on the skirts of Gandhamádana one of the monutainous barriers of Meru.*

†*Strains without.*

Soft voices low sound in the Sky,
 Where the nymphs a companion deplore;
And lament as together they fly
 The friend they encounter no more.

* This Act is without a parallell in any of the *Dramas* yet encountered. It is almost entirely in *Prákrit*, and the Prákrit is arranged, not only in metrical forms peculiar to that language, but, according to particular musical rhythm, as intended to be sung. Again, there are stage directions for the measure to which certain gesticulations are to be performed, so that it partakes both of the Operatic and Melo Dramatic character—the names of the airs and measures are not current in the present day, nor known to the Pundits—the explanations of them in the *Tika*, or Commentary on the Drama, are quoted usually from *Bharata*, whose rules no longer exist, in a collective form. The manuscript however being full of errors, little assistance has been derived in this respect from the annotator, but his definitions of the airs seem to be extracted chiefly from the *Sangita Retnákara*, from which authority it appears, that this subject has yet been very insufficiently investigated, as the modifications of the 6 *Rágas* amounted to 264, with the whole of which we are yet unacquainted—*Soma* enumerates, according to Sir William Jones, nine hundred and sixty variations. A. R. 3. 71.

† The expression is *Akshiptiká* and as a musical term implies, *Air*—the adaptation of notes, or their names, to poetical rhythm. It is said in the *Sangita Retnákara* to be arranged in the *Chachchatputa*, and other

So, sad and melodious awakes
The plaint of the Swan o'er the Stream,
Where the red Lotus blossoms, as breaks
On the wave, the day's orient beam.

ENTER *Chitralekhá and Sahajanyá.**

Chitr. (*Looking up*)
The swans along the Stream that sail
A fond companion's loss bewail—
In murmuring Songs they vent their grief,
Or find from tender tears, relief.

Saha. Now *Chitralekhá* what has chanced to cloud
Your countenance—it indicates your heart
Is ill at ease—what causes your distress

Chitr. It is not all unknown to you—engaged
Amidst our band in paying wonted service
To the all seeing Sun, I have not shared
The vernal sports—my *Urvasí* away.

tálas—(time or measure) to admit the three *Márgas* (modes) and to combine notes with words. *Bharata* adds, as cited by the commentator, it serves to introduce characters on the stage: as a measure of verse it appears both here and elsewhere, as a verse of four *pádas* or lines, the first and third containing 12 Syllables, the second 18, and fourth 15—it is the regular *Arya* or *Gáthá*, and as considered as of two lines, or hemistichs, consists of 30 and 27 Syllabic instants.

* With *Dwipadiká* is the stage direction: this measure differs from the *Dwipadi* noticed by Mr. Colebroke (A R 10-400). It is said to comprehend four kinds *Suddhá*, *Khandá*, *Mátra* and *Sampurná*, of which the first consists of 4 equal lines of 13 Syllables each, arranged in three feet—it corresponds precisely with the *Avalambaka* of Colebrooke A R 10 467, Species 52: like the preceding it is *Gítivisésha*—a kind of Song or Air.

Saha. This we all know, and know your mutual love.
Chitr. Whilst dwelling on her memory—anxious to learn
Some tidings of her, I employed my power
Of bringing absent objects to my view;
And by this art I learn what much alarms me.
Saha. Say on.
Chitr. The king, by *Urvasi's* persuasions,
Resigned of late the reins of rule, and sought
With her the groves of *Gandhamádana.**
Saha. Amid such lovely scenes, the amorous pair
Would most enjoy each other's company—
What followed.
Chitr. Whilst wandering pleasantly along the brink
Of the *Mandákini,* a nymph of air,
Who gambolled in the crystal wave, attracted
The Monarch's momentary glance—and this
Aroused the jealous wrath of *Urvasí.*

* The *Gandhamádana* mountain is one of the four boundary mountains enclosing the central region of the world called *Ilavritta,* in which the golden mountain of the Gods or Meru is situated. The *Puránas* are rather at variance as to its position, according to the *Váyu Purána* it lies on the West, connecting *Níla* and *Nishadha* the North and South ranges. The *Vishnu Purána* places it on the South — the Western mountain being there called *Vipula.* It has, however, a *Gandhamádana* to the West amongst the projecting branches or filaments of Meru. The *Bhágavat* places it on the East of Meru. The *Mahábhárat* agrees with the *Váyu Purána.* The *Padma Purana* is at variance with itself, and places it in one passage on the West and in another describes it as on the East; according to this *Purána, Kuvera* resides on it with the *Apsarasas, Gandherbas,* and *Rakshasas.* The *Sitá* alighting on its top thence descends to the *Bhadraswa versha* and flows to the Eastern Sea.

Saha. 'Tis ever thus—true love is most intolerant.
Yet destiny is mightier.
Chitr. Thus incensed,
My friend disdainfully repelled her Lord.
In sooth her mind was darkened by the curse
The Sage ere while denounced, and troubled thus,
She heedlessly forgot the law that bars
All female access from the hateful groves
Of *Kártikeya*. Trespassing the bounds
Proscribed, she suffers now the penalty
Of her transgression, and to a slender vine
Transformed, there pines till time shall set her free—
Saha. How vain the hope to shun the will of fate.
What other cause could interrupt a love
So fervent.—Where is now the king.
Chitr. He roams,
Frantic with sorrow, through the wood, in search
Of his lost bride, nor night nor day desists
From the sad quest. These rising clouds that teach
Passion to pious Sages, augur ill
For his alleviation—I much fear
There is but lttle hope of remedy—
(Repeats the first Stanza.
The Swans along the Stream that sail &c.)*

* With a slight variation of the words in the third line of the Stanza, affecting however neither the sense nor the measure—this modification of the *Dwipadika* is termed *Jambhálikä*—the *Prakrit* is as follows:

Săhăări | dūbā | līddhà—ām |
Sărăvără | āmmi Sīnī | ddhă—ām |
1st time, Vāhōv | ăgī ām | nă ă nă ām |
2d time, Avīrălă | vāhă jă | lollă ām |
Tāmmäī | Hānsī | jügălă-äm |

Saha. But think you there is no expedient then
To re-unite these Lovers.
Chitr. There is but one.
The sacred gem that owes its ruby glow
To the bright tint of *Gaurí's** sacred feet
Alone effects their union.
Saha. Let us hope it—
Their delicate forms endure not agony
Violent and protracted, and the Gods
Can surely never purpose such a pair
Should wholly perish—they will soon devise
Some means of their relief—to their high power
We leave them.—Come. The glorious Sun reveals
His countenance—let us depart and pay
Our wonted adorations. (*Sings.*)

† Amidst the wide lake—where the Lotus expands
And beauty and fragrance imparts to the Stream,
The stately swans gliding in frolicksome bands,
Unfold their white plumes in the day's dawning beam.

Exeunt.

Thus interpreted Sanscritice—*Hansi yugalam támyate*—(*Kimbhútam*) *Váshpápavalita nayanam*—or *Avirala Váshpa-jalen ollolam*—also *Sarovarasya ambhasi*, *Snigdham* and *Sahachari dukháliddham*—this will afford a specimen of the *Prakrit* of this Play and the mode in which this dialect is usually explained by the annotators, the Prosody of the *Suddhá Dwipadiká* may also be understood from the example.

* *Durgá* or *Parvati* the bride of *Siva*,

† The measure of this is termed *Khándadhará*; it is a Stanza of four *Padas* of 14 Syllables each: it is in fact the second species of the *Dwipadiká* differing from the first only by the addition of a short Syllable, as Chĩntã, dũmmĭă, mánĭăsĭá' &c.

ANOTHER PART OF THE FOREST.*

(Strains without.)

AIR.

The lord of the Elephant train,
Now wanders afar ſrom his mate:
And franticly comes to complain
To the Woods, of his desolate state.
Distraction alone for his guide,
He plunges amidst the dark bowers;
And he casts his rich trappings aside
For garlands of wild forest flowers.

ENTER *Purúravas hastily—looking up to the heavens, his dress disordered, and his general appearance indicative of insanity.*

Hold treacherous fiend, suspend thy flight, forbear—
Ah! Whither has he borne my beauteous bride:
And now his arrows sting me—thick as hail
From yonder peak whose sharp top pierces heaven,
They shower upon me.

(Rushes forward as to the attack—then pauses and looks upwards.†)

AIR.

The lonely Cygnet breasts the flood,
Without his mate, in mournful mood.

* Or in the text the *Pravésaska* the introducer—either a person on the stage, or near it who occasionally interposes to let the audience know who is coming when none of the characters perform that duty: the annunciation is in the same metre as the first, the *Akshiptiká.*

† With *Dwipadiká*, on which the *Prakrit* Stanza described in a preceding note, follows—being it may be inferred, sung.

His Snowy plumage drooping lies
And trickling tears suffuse his eyes.

It is no demon—but a friendly cloud
No hostile quiver—but the bow of Indra:
The cooling rain-drops fall, not barbed Shafts,
And I mistake the lightning for my love.

(Faints—then revives and rising.)*

AIR.†

I madly thought a fiend conveyed
Away from me, my fawn eyed maid:
The early rain-drops sense restore
To teach me to despair the more.*

Where can she bend her steps—her native gentleness
Cannot thus cherish anger—if she seek
The Skies, her love for me will soon revive.
Once mine again, not all the Demon host
That brave the Gods, should force her from my arms.
Alas, no more my gaze delighted dwells
Upon her loveliness—How sad the chance.
Fate heaps calamities with diligent malice
On those whom once misfortune has assailed.
Hence have I lost my love, when genial airs
And overshadowing clouds, veiling the day,
Had shed intenser rapture on her presence.

* *Dwipadika.*

† *Charchari*, a Stanza of which no definition is given, and which subsequently recurs in different forms: it is here a Stanza of four lines of which the three first contain 21 syllabic instants and the last 19 or 20: as a kind of song it is sung in the *Druta* or *Madhya Layas* (*Allegro* or *Allegretto*) and in either class of *Tálas* or airs called *Pratimándáka* or *Rásaka*, as with the *Láládilála* which is commonly called according to *Bharata*, *Saurasa*: *Pratimandakam Laládi Tálo loke Saurása iti abhidhiyate.*

AIR.

Ye clouds whose ceaseless torrents shed,
New glories through the gloomy air;
Awhile your angry showers forbear
Nor burst upon this humbled head—
Give me to find my love, and then fullfill
Your wrath—content I bow me to your will.

Away with this humility—the wise
Call kings the Lords of time—I will assert
My power, and bid the seasons stay their course.

AIR.*

The tree of heaven invites the breeze,
And all its countless blossoms glow;
They dance upon the gale; the bees
With sweets inebriate murmuring low,
Soft music lend, and gushes strong
The *Koïl's* deep thick warbling song.

No, I will not arrrest the march of time
For all around behold my state apparelled—
The clouds expand my canopy—their lightnings
Gleam as its glittering fringe—Rich chowries wave
Of many coloured hues from flowering trees.
The shrieking Peafowl, clamorous in their joy,
Are the loud heralds of a Sovereigns' honours—
And those bright torrents, flashing o'er the brows
Of the tall mountains, are the wealthy streams
Poured forth profuse from tributary realms.
Fye on it—what have I do with pomp—

* Also *Charchari* but a different measure. The two first lines containing each 16 *kalás* and the two last 23 each.

And kingly pride—my sole sad business here
To thread the woods in search of my beloved.

AIR.*

The monarch of the woods
With slow desponding gait
Wanders through vales and floods,
And rocks and forest bowers,
Gemmed with new springing flowers,
And mourns heart-broken for his absent mate.*
Ah me! whatever I view but aggravates
My woe—These bright and pendulous flowers
Surcharged with dew, resemble those dear eyes
Glistening with starting tears. How shall I learn
If she have passed this way—the yielding soil
Softened by showers, perchance may have retained
The delicate impression of her feet,

* *Charchari*, a verse of two lines of 32 *Kalás* or a Stanza of four divisions of sixteen syllabic moments, being the same as the *Aryagiti* of Colebrooke A. R. 10. 461. It is accompanied with some curious additions, *Páthasyante Bhinnaka*. *Bhinnaka* is called in the commentary a *Rága*; *Pátha*, is explained *Vádya—Utkara*, implying possibly instrumental prelude or *Symphony—Bhinnaka* is described as being composed in the *Madhyama gráma*, major mode, as evolved from *Shadja*, but the manuscript is here very imperfect: it is said to be adapted to the expression of heroism and surprise, to be restricted to the latter part of the day, and to be under the tutelary superintendance of *Soma*.

† At the end of the air, the Stage direction is *Dwipadikáyá parikramya avalokyacha*, having walked round the Scene, and surveyed it, with *Dwipadiká*, by which must be understood, time merely, or musical accompaniment, for the Monologue proceeds in Sanscrit, and for a short way in Prose.

And shew some vestige of their ruby tincture.*
Where in this lonely thicket may I hope
To gain some tidings of her—Yon proud Bird
Perched on the jutting crag that stately stands,
With neck outstretched and speading tail to tell
His raptures to the clouds—haply may give
Some kind intelligence.

AIR.†

The royal elephant the dread
Of all his rival foes;
With downcast eye and tardy tread,
Through tangled thickets goes;
To solitary grief a prey,
His loved companion far away.

AIR.‡

I will speak to this Peacock—oh tell
If, free on the wing as you soar,

* The soles being stained with the red juice of the *Mehndi.*

† *Khandaka*, a verse of four lines the two first containing twelve *kalás* the two last 14: it may be one of the many varieties of the *Atyagiti* measure, also called *Khandaka* (A R 10.46 the two short lines contain three feet, the two long four, and all but the first foot of the first line which is a spondee and the first of the third and fourth, which are pyrrhics, are anapæsts as

Sāmpāt | tă vĭsū | rănăō | tŭ-
rĭyām | părăvā | rănă-ō |
Pĭă | dămă dān | sănălā | lăsă-ō
Găă | vără vī | hmĭă mā | năsă-ō

‡ The direction here is *Tena Khandakánte Charchari.* The *Charchari* is a long Stanza, the four lines consisting each of 22 Syllabic moments or *Kalás*—*Tena* is a mystical prefix to verses, according to the commentator, an auspicious inceptive particle explained by *Bharata*, as here cited, to signify *by*

In forest, or meadow, or dell,
You have seen the loved nymph I deplore—
You will know her, the fairest of damsels fair
By her large soft eye, and her graceful air.

(Advancing to the bird and bowing.)*

Bird of the dark blue throat and eye of jet
Oh tell me have you seen the lovely face
Of my fair bride—lost in this dreary wilderness:
Her charms deserve your gaze—how—no reply
He answers not, but beats a measure—how—
What means this merry mood—Oh yes I know
The cause—he now may boast his plumage
Without a peer, nor shame to shew his glories
Before the floating tresses of my *Urvasi.*
I leave him, nor will waste a thought on one
Who feels no pity for another's woes

(Proceeds; Music†)

Yonder amidst the thick and shady branches
Of the broad *Jambu,* cowers the *Koïl*—faint
Her flame of passion in the hotter breath
Of noon; she of the birds is wisest famed—
I will address her.‡

Brahme or God, analogous to the import of *Tad in Tat-twam-asi.* That all pervading Spirit thou art—and similar phrases, and should be prefixed to Airs.

* With *Charcharikà*—here of course something different from the *Charchari* which is sung—*Bharata* is cited to call it either a sort of measured movement or measure, *Jati* or *Tála*, which consists of two *Druta* and eight *Laghu* (notes) which it perhaps is allowable to call two quavers and eight crotchets.

† With *Dwipadika.*

‡ *Khuruka* a sort of dance or gesticulation to musical measure; the name is also applied to a particular combination of of letters or figure of rhetoric.

AIR.*

Majestic as sails the mighty cloud
Along the dusky air,
The Elephant cometh hither to shroud
In the thickets his despair.
From his heart all hope of delight is riven
And his eyes with tears o'erflow,
As he roams the shades, where the sons of heaven
Descend to sport below.

AIR.†

Say nurseling of a stranger nest,‡
Say hast thou chanced a nymph to see,
Amidst these gardens of the blest,
Wandering at liberty;
Or warbling with a voice divine
Melodious strains more sweet than thine.
(Approaches and kneels.)
Sweet Bird—whom lovers deem Love's messenger,||
Skilled to direct the God's envenomed shafts,
And tame the proudest heart; oh hither guide
My lovely fugitive, or lead my steps
To where she strays.(*turns to his left,*¶*and as if replying*)

* *Charchari* of 42 and 36, or 21. 21. 18. and 18, syllabic instants.

† With *Valantiká*, described in the *Sangita Retnákara*, as an *Upánga* or sub-division of a *Rága*: it is here of course the melody or strain.

‡ The *Köil*, like the Cuckoo is said to leave its eggs in the nests of other birds.

|| Because the *Koil's* song is especially heard at the season of spring the friend of love.

¶ This sort of turn however even is technical, and is termed *Vámaka*.

Why did she leave
One so devoted to her will? In wrath
She left me, but the cause of anger lives not
In my imagination—the fond tyranny
That women exercise o'er those who love them
Brooks not the slightest shew of disregard.
How now: the Bird has flown—'tis ever thus—
All coldly listen to another's sorrows.
Unheeding my affliction, lo, she speeds
Intent on joy expected, to yon tree,
To banquet on the luscious juice, the *Jambu**
From its now ripe and roseate fruit distills.
Like my beloved, the Bird of tuneful song
Deserts me; let her go—I can forgive her

(Proceeds—Music.)

Ha—on my right—amidst the wood I hear
A tinkling melody——'tis the sweet chime
My fair one's anklets echo to her footsteps.

AIR†

Through the woods the stately elephant strays,
And his glances despair express;

* The Rose apple so denominated from its odour: it is however the *Mahájambu* that is mentioned in the text.

† *Kakubha* a *Rága*, according to *Bharata*—*Kakubhá* appears a *Rágini* in the list quoted by Sir Wm. Jones from Mirza Khan but it differs in gender and denomination, (A. R. 3 81) the passage is not very clear in the manuscript, either of the Comment or *Sangita Retnakara*, but the *Kakubha* is a form in the mode of *Dhaivata* of which *Dha* is the Ansa or key note. The notation of the Scale is given by Sir W. Jones *Dha-ni-sa-ri-ga-ma-pa*. The *Rága* is called the *Shadupabhanga*, or

On his limbs the enfeebling malady preys,
And his steps are slow with distress;
In his eyes the starting tear drop swells,
As his thought on his lost companion dwells

Alas, the gathering of the clouds deceives
The swan, who hails rejoicingly the time
For periodic flight to *Mánasa.**
I hear his song of gladness not the sound
Of tinkling anklets—ere yet the troop begins
Its distant march I will address the chief.
Ho—Monarch of the tribes that breast the stream,
Forbear awhile your course: forego the provender
Of Lotus stems, not needed yet, and hear
My suit—redeem me from despair—impart
Some tidings of my love—'tis worthier far
To render kindly offices to others
Than meanly labour for a selfish good—
He heeds me not, but still on *Mánasa*
Intent, collects his store—and now I note him
More closely, I suspect some mystery.
Why seek to veil the truth—if my beloved
Was never seen by thee as graceful straying
Along the flowery borders of the lake,
Then whence this elegant gait—'Tis hers—and thou
Hast stolen it from her—in whose every step
Love sports—thy walk betrays thee; own thy crime,

in six parts and the verse has six lines--the rhythm both of the air and poetry being thus irregularly subdivided as more expressive of a disordered imagination--it is followed by a Stanza of the *Dwipadika* class, four lines of 14 *Kalás* each, which repeating the same ideas has been omitted.

And lead me quickly to her. *(laughs)* Nay he fears
Our Royal power—the plunderer flies the king.

Proceeds—Music.

Yonder I see the *Chakwa** with his mate;
Of him I will enquire

AIR.†

In groves of tall trees with bright blossoms blooming
And vocal with many sweet murmured tones,
The Lord of the herd whom grief is consuming
Distracted the loss of his mate bemoans.

AIR. *After a pause.*‡

Ah no, he replies, I taste on the wing,
The joys of the cool returning spring,
And as each feather thrills with delight,
I mark not the fair that meet my sight.

Yet tell me—hast thou seen her—know'st thou not
Who asks thy answer—the great king of day
And monarch of the night are my progenitors:

* The *Chakra váka* or *Ruddy* goose: these birds are supposed to be separated through the night.

† Here the gesture is described; *Kutilika* with which it is directed to begin, being explained, standing with the feet something apart, the left hand extended and the right resting on the hip. In the second line of the Stanza the gesture is changed to *Mallaghati* and in the two last to *Charchari*, the Stanza is *Dwipadika* four lines of 14 Syllables each.

‡ *Dwilayántaré* after two *Layas*, the commentator cites *Amerá's* explanation of *Laya*—which is the concurrence in time of voice, instrument, and gesticulation, here however it must imply something else, an interval probably, or a definite measure of symphony or prelude.

Their grandson I, and by their own free choice,
The Lord of *Urvasi* and of the Earth.
How-silent—thou might'st measure my affliction
By what thou feelest; all the air resounds
With thy incessant plaints, if, but a moment
Thy fair companion nestling hides in sport
Amongst the lotus leaves, and flies thy view.
Alas—to one whom fate has cursed like me
Nought is propitious—I will ask no more.

Proceeds—Music.

How beautiful the lotus—it arrests
My path and bids me gaze on it—the bees
Murmur amidst its petals—like the lip
Of my beloved it glows, when that has been
Somewhat too rudely sipped by mine, and long
Retains the amorous impress—I will woo
This honey rifler to become my friend

*Advances.**

AIR.

Unheeding the cygnet at first,
His beak in the nectar of passion dips;
But fiercer and fiercer his thirst—
As deeper he sips.

Say plunderer of the honied dew—hast thou
Beheld the nymph whose large and languid eye
Voluptuous rolls as if it swam with wine.
And yet methinks 'tis idle to enquire,

* With the *Ardhadwichaturasraka*, a particular mode of gesticulating, this is changed at the end of the *Prákrit* verse to *Dwichaturasraka*—a term of like import.

For had he tasted her delicious breath
He now would scorn the lotus—I will hence.

*Proceeds—Music.**

Beneath the shade of yon *Kadamba* tree
The royal elephant reclines, and with him
His tender mate—I will approach—yet hold
From his Companion he accepts the bough
Her trunk has snapped from the balm breathing tre
Now rich with teeming shoots and juicy fragrance.

Advances† then Pauses.‡

He crushes it—I may proceed

AIR

King of the forest whose sports have felled
The stateliest trees, the thicket's pride;
Oh, say, in these shades hast thou beheld,
More bright than the Moon, my wandering bride.

Advancing a few paces.

Chief of the mighty herd—say hast thou seen
My love—like the young moon her delicate frame,
And with eternal youth her beauties glow;
Her voice is music—her long tresses wear
The Jasmine's|| golden hue, hadst thou afar
Beheld her charms they must have fixed thy gaze.

* *Dwipadikayá Parikrámitakena* is the stage direction.

† *Sthánakena*; and *Sthánaka* is identified with a variety of *Alápa* on the authority of *Bharata*---*Alápa* appears in the *Sangita Retnakara* to signify modulation, the succession of notes conformably to a fixed scale, but no determined measure.

‡ In the original he commences a Stanza to the *Kutilika* measure, but breaks off abruptly.

|| *Yuthiká savala kesi*, having hair brown as the yellow *Jasmine--golden* or *auburn*. a very strange idea for a Hindu:

Ha, he replies. That kind assenting roar
Conveys some intimation—oh repeat
The sound—consider that we should befriend
Each other, bound by various common ties.
Thou art the sovereign of the forest—Me
They term the King of men. Thy bounty sheds
Thy frontal fragrance on the air, my wealth
On all is showered profuse—Amongst the bands
Of lovely nymphs obedient to my will
One only *Urvasi* commands my love,
As thou hast chosen this, thy favourite
From all the herd. Thus far our fates accord,
And never be the pangs of separation,
Such as distract my bosom, known to thee,
Propitious be thy fortunes; friend, farewell.

Proceeds.

What have we here . deep in the mountain's breast
A yawning chasm appears: such shades are ever
Haunts of the nymphs of air and earth. Perchance
My *Urvasi* now lurks within the grotto
In cool seclusion---I will enter---All
Is utter darkness. Would the lightning's flash
Now blaze to guide me---no---the cloud disdains,
Such is my fate perverse, to shed for me,
It's many channelled radiance—be it so
I will retire—but first the rock address.

it is said that in the west of India such hair is sometimes seen, but the prejudice in favour of ebon locks is so strong that it is considered a morbid affection of the hair, and the women dye and conceal it.

Air.*

With horny hoofs and a resolute breast
The boar through the thicket stalks;
He ploughs up the ground, as he plies his quest
In the forest's gloomiest walks.

Say mountain whose expansive slope confines
The forest verge, oh tell me hast thou seen
A fair nymph, straining up thy steep ascent,
Or wearied resting in thy crowning woods
That Love delights to make his shady dwelling—
How, no reply, remote he hears me not—
I will approach him nearer.

Air.†

From thy crystal summits the glistening springs
Rush down the flowery sides—
And the spirit of heaven delightedly sings
As among thy peaks he hides.
Say mountain so favoured have the feet
Of my fair one pressed this calm retreat.

Now by my hopes he answers—he has seen her—
Where is she—say : alas ! again deceived—
Alone I hear the echo of my words
As round the cavern's hollow mouth they roll
And multiplied return—ah *Urvasí*—(*faints*).

(*Recovers and sits as exhausted.*)

Fatigue has overcome me—I will rest

* *Khandiká* a kind of song in the *Kumbhatála* time—or the verse is a Stanza of two lines of 26 Syllabic moments each.

† *Charchari*, a Stanza four lines 17 syllabic instants each.

Upon the borders of this mountain torrent,
And gather vigour from the breeze that gleans
Refreshing coolness from its gelid waves.
Whilst gazing on the stream, whose new swoln waters
Yet turbid flow, what strange imaginings
Possess my soul and fill it with delight.
The rippling wave is like her arching brow,
The fluttering line of storks her timid tongue,
The foamy spray her white loose floating vest,
And this meandering course the current tracks
Her undulating gait; all these recall
My soon-offended love—I must appease her

AIR.*

Be not relentless, dearest.
Nor wrath with me for ever.
I mark where thou appearest
A fair and mountain river.

Like *Ganga* proud thou shewest,
From heavenly regions springing;
Around thee as thou flowest
The birds their course are winging.

The timid deer confiding
Thy flowery borders throng;
And Bees, their store providing,
Pour forth enraptured song.

* *Kutiliká*, as formerly occurring, gesticulation, but it should here rather imply metre: the verse is a Stanza of 4 lines of 16 syllabic instants, and is of the *Arya Giti* class.

AIR.*

In the lowering East the king of the deep
Expects his coming bride;
His limbs are the clouds that darkly sweep
The skirts of the heaving tide;
And his tossing arms are the tumbling waves,
Where the gale o'er the heaving billow raves.

With rapture he dances, the Lord of the main,
And proud in his state appears:
His steps are pursued by the monster train
The deep Sea darkness rears;
And the curlew, the swan, and glistening shell
And the lotus, the monarch's glory swell.

The bellowing surges his fame resound,
And dash at the gates of heaven,
The sea with the sky they threat to confound,
But back with shame are driven;
For now the young Rains are armed for their right
And their prowess arrests old ocean's might

(Approaches and bows.)

Oh nymph adored, what crime have I committed,
That thus you fly from one so wholly yours,
Who now implores your pity, and with terror
Anticipates your loss—relent—return——
This is not *Urvasí.* She would not quit me
Even for the Ocean King—What's to be done—

* *Charchari*, 6 lines of 22 syllabic instants each: it is very much expanded in the translation, being in the original exceedingly brief and obscure.

Fortune crowns those who yield not to despair—
I'll back to where my love first disappeared.
Yonder the black Deer couchant lies; of him
I will enquire – Ho Antelope*—behold
The royal elephant *Airávata*†
Scorched by the pangs of solitude explores
In search of his lost mate, the groves of *Nandana*;‡
Whose close embowering walks are resonant
With the glad *Koils* song, as pleased he sips
The juicy nectar of the clustering blossoms.
How—he averts his gaze—as he disdained
To hear my suit—ah no— he anxious marks
His doe approach him—tardily she comes,
Her frolic fawn impending her advance

AIR.||

A nymph of heaven has left her sphere
To make a heavenly region here,
And treads this sacred ground.
Her slender waist, her swelling hips,
Her languid eye, her ruby lips
With youth unfading crowned.
Oh tell me through the tangled maze,
If wandering she has met thy gaze,
Deer of the soft black eye—
Ere yet beneath the yawning brink

* Advancing with *Galantiká*, termed merely a kind of *nátya* dance or gesticulation.

† The elephant of *Indra*: this illustration proceeds unlike all the preceding, in Sanscrit, in the usual measure.

‡ The Garden of *Indra*.

|| *Charchari*, a verse of four lines of 22 syllabic instants each.

Of sorrow's gulph, immersed I sink
Befriend me, or I die—

Advances.

Lord of the bounding herds, say hast thou seen
My fair whose large and languid eye resembles
That of thy tender mate—he heeds me not—
But springs to meet his doe—be happy both
Though fate still adverse frown on my desires.

Proceeds and pauses.

How now—what stream of ruddy radiance breaks
Through the cleft rock—no flame could have survived
The fast descending torrents—'tis perchance
Some sanguine fragment of the Lion's feast.
No—'tis a gem—more roseate than the blush
Of the *Asoka* blossoms, and the Sun
Would grasp it with his beams—it pleases me
And I will make it mine.

AIR.*

With tearful eye and dejected gaze,
Despairing his Love to meet;
All lonely the Royal Elephant strays
Through the forest's still retreat.
Why should I take the jewel. She whose brow
Bound with *Mandára* fillets, best had worn
The costly gem, is far—far from me—why
Should I distain the ruby with my tears.

* *Dwipadiká*, four lines fourteen *kalás* each.

—Going—a Voice in the air.—

Take up the gem, my Son; its radiant red
The feet of *Hema's* holy daughter shed*
And wonderous virtue gave—let it adorn
Thy hand and thou wilt shortly cease to mourn
Thy absent bride—once more by this restored
To bless her sorrowing and lamented Lord.

Pur. What voice is this—descends some friendly sage
In pity of my griefs, or in some deer
Disguised, directs me thus. Seer—I obey
And thank thy holy counsel—Gem divine
Restore me to my love, and I will bear thee
High on my diadem, and hold thee ever
As dear as *Iswara* his crescent moon—

—Takes the gem and proceeds, then pauses—

What means this strange emotion—as I gaze
Upon this vine—no blossoms deck its boughs;
Nipped by the falling rains, like briny tears,
The buds have perished, and the mournful shrub
All unadorned appears to pine in absence—
No bees regale her with their songs—silent
And sad, she, lonely, shews the image
Of my repentant love, who now laments
Her causeless indignation—I will press
The melancholy likeness to my heart—

* *Gauri* or *Párvati*, the stone is fabled to have received its colour, and virtues from contact with the soles of her feet stained with the red of the Mehndi (*Lawsonia inermis.*)

AIR.

Vine of the wilderness, behold,
A lone heart-broken wretch in me,
Who dreams in his embrace to fold
His love, as wild he clings to thee.
And might relenting fate restore
To these fond arms the nymph I mourn;
I'd bear her hence, and never more
To these forbidden haunts return.

(Goes to embrace the Creeper which is transformed to Urvasí)*

What can this mean, through every fibre spreads,
The conscious touch of *Urvasí*—yet all
I deemed her charms deceived me—let me wake
And realise the vision or dispell it.
'Tis no deceit—'Tis she—my best beloved—*(faints.)*

Urv. *(in tears.)* Glory to the King—

Pur. *(reviving.)* Thy loss dear love has plunged my sinking spirit
Deep into dreariest gloom; but now thy sight
Arrests my soul, and calls me back to bliss.

Urv. I knew not of your woe, myself deprived
Of conscious being

Pur. How—what mean you—speak

Urv. I will explain, but let me first implore
Forgiveness, that my causeless wrath has wrought
So sad a change in you.

Pur. Enough, enough;
You mine once more, all else is quite forgotten,

* Or, enters as it were in its very place, *Tatah pravisati tat sthane eva Urvasi.*

And every thought is extasy—but come
Say how you cheered your time, your lord away—
For me—

AIR.*

I have sued to the starry plumed Bird,
And the *Koil* of love-breathing song;
To the Lord of the Elephant herd,
And the Bee as he murmured along:
To the Swan, and the loud Waterfall,
To the *Chakwa,* the Rock and the Roe,
In thy search have I sued to them all,
But none of them lightened my woe.

Urv. To me—all news of my lamented lord
Came but in fond imaginings

Pur. How thus—

Urv. In ancient days, the warrior God adopted
A cœnobites observance—and for this
Retiring to the woods that stud the vale
Of *Gandhamádana,* then called *Akalusha,*
He framed this law.

Pur. What law—proceed—

Urv. The female that should rashly pass the bounds
Proscribed, and penetrate the forest shades,
Should instant metamorphose undergo,
And to a twining shrub should be transformed—
Alone from such sad change to be redeemed,
By the celestial gem, whose ruby glow
Is gleaned from *Gauri's* foot. This law I broke—

* *Charchari.*

Bewildered by the Sage's imprecation
I thoughtless plunged into the thicket's glooms
Shunned ever by the gods, and in a vine
My form and faculties awhile were lost.

Pur. 'Tis all explained; no ordinary cause
I knew detained thee from me: thee, whose fears
Brooked not my momentary separation,
Even in thy dreams—The virtue of the gem,
As thou hast said, this day effects our meeting.
Behold it here.

Urv. The Ruby of Reunion,
This holy gem restores me to my nature.
(Takes it and puts it respectfully to her forehead)

Pur. A moment thus; let me behold thy brow,
Irradiated by this heavenly jewel
Like the red lotus ere its buds expand.

Urv. The king delights to flatter me, but now
Let us return to *Pratishthána;* long
The city mourns its absent lord, and I
The cause of his departure, shall incur,
The angry censures of the people: come—
How will it please you travel—

Pur. Yonder cloud
Shall be our downy car, to waft us swift
And lightly on our way—the lightnings wave
Its glittering banners, and the bow of Indra
Hangs as its overarching canopy
Of variegated and resplendent hues.

AIR.

The ardent swan his mate recovers
And all his spirit is delight:

With her aloft in air he hovers,
And homeward wings his joyous flight.

[*Exeunt on the cloud; music.**

END OF THE FOURTH ACT.

ACT V.

THE PALACE OF PURURAVAS

Enter Mánavaka

At last thank the fates, the king has returned with Madam *Urvasi* from the groves of *Nandana*, the pleasant gardens of the Gods. My friend is once more attentive to his royal duties and the cares of state—yet he seems out of spirits—what should be the cause—except the want of children he has nothing to grieve for—This is a bustling day—the king and his queens have just performed their royal ablutions where the *Yamuná* and the Ganges meet : he must be at his toilet by this time, and by joining him I shall secure a share of the flowers and perfumes prepared for him.

(*Noise behind*) The Ruby—the ruby—a hawk taking it for a piece of flesh has borne away the Ruby of Reunion from the plaintain leaf, on which it was a moment placed along with the Lady's robes.

* With *Khandadhará* a sort of air—maintaining the curious character of this act to the last—the actor who could execute the monologue with all its airs must be endowed with extraordinary powers.

Man. Here's a pretty piece of work—the jewel my friend so highly prized—Ho, here he comes, not yet attired—I will keep aloof.

Enter Purúravas in haste followed by the Chamberlain, a hunter and attendants.*

Pur. Where is the winged thief that rashly courts
His own destruction, and presumes to violate
The dwelling of his Sovereign.

Hunter. Yonder he goes—the golden chain of the jewel hanging from his beak.

Pur. I see him—as he rapid flies around
In airy rings, the whirling chain appears
To hem him in a fiery circle—
What's to be done.

Man. (*Advancing.*) Punish him to be sure, put the culprit to death.

Pur. Bring me my bow. (*A female attendant* goes out and returns with a bow and arrows which she gives to the king.*
'Tis now too late—he flies
Far to the South beyond the arrow's reach—

* Also called a *Kiráta* a forester: the *Kirátas* the Mountaineer and Savage tribes of India were known to the ancients as the *Cirrhadæ* on the Coromandel coast—they appear to have been independant but were tributary to the Hindu kings—or perhaps only rendered personal service.

* A *Yavani* which is rather inexplicable—the *Mohammedan* Princes had guards of African women in their harams, and the presence of female attendants in those of the Hindu Sovereigns has also been adverted to, but the term *Yavani* has been applied by the later Hindus to the *Mohammedans*, and it is not likely that either Persian or Arabian women ever found their way into the inner appartments of Hindu princes, as personal

Red as *Asoka* flowers the precious gem
Graces the sky—with sullen fires it glows
Like angry Mars, bursting at intervals
Through the thick clouds that overhang the night.
My good *Látavya.* (*to the Chamberlain.*) give command, the Bird
Be tracked, and followed to his perch.

Cham. The king shall be obeyed. [*Exit.**

Man. Now please you sit—the thief will not be able to escape your power.

Pur. (*Sits.*) Were it an ordinary gem its loss
Would move me not—but to lose this would vex me—
To it I owe reunion with my love.

Man. Well there is this comfort; as you have the lady, you are no longer in need of the jewel.

ENTER *the Chamberlain with an Arrow and the Jewel.*

Cham. Victory to your grace! the bird condemned by your Majesty's decree has fallen, pierced by this Shaft—the ruby is recovered; it has been cleansed with water; please you say to whom it shall be intrusted.

attendants or guards. If, as has been supposed, *Yavanas* formerly implied Greeks, it is equally impossible that Greek women should have fulfilled such an office, as few could have found their way to India, or even to Bactria, and those would have been, it may be supposed, too highly valued by their Countrymen to have been suffered to act as slaves to Barbarians—perhaps Tartarian or Bactrian women may be intended.

* There is evidently much more art in the conduct of the business in this piece than in the Toy Cart. The Chamberlain would there have been sent out, and would have returned immediately, in all probability, instead of any dialogue filling up the interval.

Pur. Ho, Forester, let the gem
Be purified with flame, and then replace it
Safe in its casket.

Hunter—As your Majesty commands.

[*Exit. the Kiráta or Forester.*

Pur. Know you to whom the Shaft belongs.

Cham. There is a name inscribed upon it your grace, but my eye sight cannot distinguish the characters.

Pur. Let me see them.

(*Takes the arrow and expresses wonder and delight.*)

Cham. With your grace's leave I will now attend to other duties. [*Exit.*

Man. What does your majesty study so intently.

Pur. Listen—" The arrow of the all subduing *Ayus,*
The son of *Urvasí* and *Purúravas.*"

Man. Joy to your grace. Fate has crowned your wishes.

Pur. How should this be—but for the interval
Of the *Naimisha** sacrificial rite
My *Urvasi* has always been with me—
I do recall indeed a transient period,
When her soft cheek was paler than the leaf
Cold-nipped and shrivelled—and her eloquent eye
Betrayed unwonted lassitude—aught else
I never noted.

Man. Oh you must not suppose that the nymphs of heaven manage these matters like those of earth—No, no—they have the power to counteract all such appearances.

* The *Naimishcya* sacrifice is the great sacrifice performed at the *Naimisha* forest by the assembled sages which lasted twelve years according to the *Mahábhárat*, a thousand according to the *Bhágavat.*

Pur. It may be so; yet why this mystery;
Why keep from me all knowledge of my child.

Man. Oh there's no accounting for the fancies of celestial Spirits.

ENTER *Chamberlain.*

Cham. So please your majesty, a saintly dame and a young lad from the hermitage of *Chyavana** solicit admittance.

Pur. Let them enter—quick.

* *Chyavana* is the Son of *Bhrigu*, the son of *Brahmá*, by his wife *Puloma*. A *Rakshasa* or fiend attempting to carry off *Pulomà* the child was prematurely born, whence his name from *Chyu* to fall from. Upon his birth his splendor was such as to reduce the insulter of his mother to ashes. *Mahábhárat Adi Parva, Pulomá Adhyáya.* The sage having adopted a life of ascetic devotion was so immersed in abstraction that he became completely covered with the nests of white ants. *Sukanyá* the daughter of king *Saryáti* wandering in the forest observed what she thought two lights in an ant hill, and thrust in two blades of *Kusa* grass, which when withdrawn were followed by a flow of blood. Much alarmed the Princess repaired to her father and related what had happened. The king conjecturing the truth immediately went to the spot to deprecate the wrath of the *Rishi*, and pacified him by giving him the damsel in marriage. After being married some time, the *Aswini Kumáras* passing by *Chyavana's* residence conferred upon him youth and beauty, in requital of which boons he gave them a share in the *Soma* juice offered at sacrifices to the gods—the Gods with *Indra* at their head opposed this grant, and *Indra* lifted up his arm to strike *Chyavana* dead with his thunbolt, when the sage paralysed his arm. To appall the Gods he created the demon *Mada*, intoxication personified, in terror of whom and of the power of the Saint, the Gods acceded to the participation of the *Aswini Kumaras* in divine honours. *Indra* was restored to the use of his arm, and *Mada* was divided and distributed amongst dice, women and wine. *Bhavishyat Purána* and the *Dána Dherma* section of the *Mahábhárat.*

Enter *a Tápasi or Female Ascetic, and a Boy with a bow in his hand.*

Man. Observe him sir—that warrior lad must be the owner of the arrow, he is your perfect image.

Pur. May it prove so – my imperfect sight,
Is dimmed with tears—my heart is overcome
With tenderness ; and strong emotions crowd
My agitated mind—on all my limbs
A sudden tremor seizes—how I long
To clasp him to my bosom.

Cham. Here pause most reverend Lady.

Pur. *(Bowing.)* Hail holy Dame.

Tap. May fortune ever wait.
The glorious line of *Soma.* *(Apart.)* Now, methinks,
The king has secret intimation given him
I bring him here his son. *(Aloud)* Boy Pay your homage.

(Ayus bows)

Puru. May your years be many.

Ayus. *(Apart)* If I dared listen to my heart—I should
Believe this were my father—I his son—
For I have never known the fond endearments
Paternal love bestows upon a child.

Puru. What brings thee to our presence saintly Dame,

Tap. Let the king hear—This princely youth, the son
Of *Urvasi,* was for some cause confided,
Without your knowledge, to my secret care.
The ceremonies of his martial birth
The pious *Chyavana* has duly ministered,
Taught him the knowledge fitted to his station

And lastly trained his growing youth to arms :*
But now my charge expires, for an act
This day achieved, unfits him to remain
An inmate of the peaceful hermitage.

Pur. What act?

Tap. Whilst on his mission with the *Rishi's* Sons,
To gather fuel, flowers and holy grass—
From the adjacent woods, he aimed a shaft
Against a hawk new perched upon a tree
With his fresh prey, and took his felon life.
This deed of blood excludes him from our haunts,
And by the Sage's orders I conduct him
Again to *Urvasî*—I would see the queen.

Puru. Be seated, and mean while *Látavyă.*
Apprise our queen, that we would see her here.

[*Exit Chamberlain.*

Puru. Come hither boy. As the moon's silver ray
Affects the lunar gem, his presence sheds
Spontaneous joy, and through each fibre darts
The consciousness that I behold my son.

Tap. Obey your Sire (*The Prince advances and prostrates himself: Purúravas raises and embraces him and places him on the footstool of his throne.*—)

* The original has *Dhanur-vidya* archery—which is always put for military science in general. That archery however was the predominant branch of the art amongst the Hindus is evident from this use of the term, and from all descriptive accounts of heroic education—*Rama*—his sons; the *Pandavas*—*Ayus* and all other princes are represented in the *Ramayana*, *Mahábhárat*, and all poems and plays as making archery a principal part of their education, furnishing a remarkable analogy in this respect to the practice of the ancient Persians, and Scythian

Pur. Salute your father's friend—Boy, fear not.

Man. What should he fear—he has seen baboons enough in the hermitage.

Ayus. (*Smiling*) Accept my homage Sir.

Man. Fortune attend you ever.

ENTER *Urvasi preceded by the Chamberlain.*

Cham. This way your grace,

Urv. (*Seeing Ayus*) What youth is this, who in the Royal presenee
Armed with the bow and quiver honoured sits
Upon the golden footstool—whilst the king
Is fondly playing with his twisted tresses.
Ha! *Satyavatí* too! it is my Son,
His growth out strips my memory,

Puru. Behold your mother, boy—her gaze intent
Is fixed upon you—and her heaving bosom
Has rent its veiling scarf.

Tap. Haste to embrace her.

(*Ayus rises and goes to his Mother who embraces him, then, after a pause.*)

Urv. Hail—holy mother,

Tap. Ever may you know,
Your lord's affection.

Ayus. Mother—accept my salutations

Urv. (*Kisses him*) My dear boy,
Be long your father's happines and pride
(*Advances*) Glory to the King

Puru. To the matron—honour,
(*Hands Urvasi to a Seat with him on the throne*)
Be seated all (*they sit*)

Tap. The princely youth is perfectly accomplished
In all the science that becomes his rank,
And is of years and strength to bear the load
Of martial mail; unfitted to the thoughts
And duties of the tranquil hermitage;
I yield him therefore, in the royal presence,
Back to his mother's arms,

Urv. And I receive him,
Most willingly: for it is no longer meet
He should disturb the quiet of devotion.
When he is satiate with his father's sight
He may revisit you, till then farewell.

Puru. And bear my reverence to the holy Sage.

Ayus. Will you not take me with you *Satyavatí.*

Tap. No my dear child—the labours of the Student
Are all performed, 'tis time you enter now
*On loftier duties—

Ayus. Well—if it must be so,
Farewell—but send me here my favourite peacock

Tap. I will, and boy, remember that you heed
Your father ever—Peace be unto all—[*Exit.*

Pur. Thus blessed, my love, with thee and with my Son,
I envy not the happiness of Indra.*

Urv. Ah me (*Weeps violently*)

Pur. What means this sudden grief?
Why when I contemplate with ecstacy
The proud perpetuation of my race,
Should these dear drops in swift succession spread
A pearly fillet on thy heaving bosom.

* Or literally, You enter now the second order, that of the householder.

† Or I think myself like *Indra* with *Paulomi* (his bride) and *Jayanta*) (his son.)

Urv. Alas, my lord, the name of *Swerga's* king
Brings to my memory a dread decree
By him denounced—which happy in the sight
Of this loved boy I had awhile forgotten—
When for your love I gladly left the courts
Of heaven, the monarch thus declared his will.
" Go and be happy with the Prince my friend,
But when he views the Son that thou shalt bear him
Then hitherward direct thy prompt return."
'Twas fear of this that bade me keep concealed
My infant's birth, and instant I conveyed him
To *Chyavana's* retreat, entrusting him
To yonder pious dame, to be instructed,
Such my pretext, in our most sacred lore.
The fated term expires, and to console
His father for my loss, he is restored—
I may no longer tarry.

Pur. Adverse fate
Is still intent to mar my perfect joy.
Scarce have I known the blessing of a son
When my fair bride is snatched from my embrace.
The tree that languished in the Summer's blaze
Puts forth reviving, as young rain descends,
Its leafy shoots, when, lo the lightning bursts,
Fierce on its top and fells it to the ground.

Man. I see nothing left for this but to abandon the throne, assume the coat of bark, and betake yourself to the forests.*

Urv. But what remains for me—my task on earth
Fulfilled—once gone the king will soon forget me.

* Such appears to have been a common practice with the princes of India when satiate with years and power, or disgusted with the world.

Pur. Dearest, not so: immersed in cares of state
I less might feel the pangs of separation.
Then be the deer trod thickets my election,
Where lonely I may long indulge my woe:
Our son shall wield the sceptre of the world.

Ayus. Excuse me Sire—my years are all unfit
For such a burthen—one so long upheld
By thy exalted merits.

Pur. Fear it not
The elephant cub* soon tames the forest herds;
The snake scarce hatched concocts the deadly poison:
Kings are in boyhood monarchs, and endowed
With powers inborn to rule the race of man;
Nature, not age, gives fitness. (*to the Chamberlain,*)
Látavya bid,
Our ministers and priests be all prepared
For this our son's inauguration—speed.

Cham. I obey.

[*Exit sorrowfully and all on the scene express grief.*

Pur. What sudden splendor breaks, whence are these flashes
Of Lightning in a cloudless sky.

Urv. 'Tis *Náreda.*

Pur. His braided curls are of a golden dye;
His sacred cord, bright as the silver moon:
Around his neck, are strings of heavenly pearl:
Like a celestial tree with glittering stem
He moves: prepare we to receive him.

Urv. Here,

* The young *Gandhagaja* soon subdues other elephants, is the expression of the original—they are said to fly the odour of some particular excretion, whence the name of the animal.

This offering of respect, gathered in haste
Present the sage.

(Gives the King some Flowers)

Náreda descends.

Nar. Triumph attend
The brave defender of this middle sphere.

Pur. *(Presenting the oblation.)* Reverence to the sage.

Urv. Accept my homage. *(Bows.)*

Nar. Never be wife and husband disunited.

Pur. *(Apart.)* Oh might this be. *(Aloud.)* Advance, my son and pay
Your adoration to the holy seer.

Ayus. *Ayus,* the son of *Urvasi,* presumes
To pay you homage. *(Bows to Nareda.)*

Nar. May your days be many—King, attend:
The mighty *Indra* to whom all is known,
By me thus intimates his high commands.
Forego your purpose of ascetic sorrow.
The sages, to whose wisdom past and future
Are as the present, have foretold at hand
Hostilities in heaven, and the Gods will need
Your prowess—then relinquish not your arms;
And *Urvasi* shall be* through life united
With thee in holy bonds.

Urv. These happy words
Extract a barbed arrow from my bosom.

Pur. Whatever *Indra* wills I shall obey.

* This is a very material variation in the story as told in the play and in the *Puranas:* the passage *Tena twayá na Sastram sannyastavyam; Iyam cha Urvasi yávadáyus távat Sahadherma chárini bhavishyati.*

Nar. 'Tis wisely said, he will not be unthankful.
The fiery element sustains the sun,
The sun returns his rays to nourish fire.

(Looking upwards.)

Rembhá appear, and bring the holy wave
Consigned by *Indra* to your charge, to consecrate
The prince's elevation to the throne—
As partner of the Empire.*

(Rembhá and other Nymphs descend with a Golden Vase containing the Water of the Heavenly Ganges, a Throne and other Paraphernalia which they arrange.)

Rem. All is prepared.

Nar. Prince, to your seat.

(Nárada leads Ayus to the Throne of Inauguration, takes the Golden Ewer from Rembhá and pours Water on the head of the Prince.)

Rembha complete the rite.

(Rembhá and the Apsarasas perform the rest of the ceremony.)†

Rem. Now Prince salute your Parents and the Sage.

(As Ayus bows to them respectively, they reply.)

Nar. Unvarying fortune wait upon thy reign.

Pur. My son, sustain the honours of your lineage.

Urv. My son, be still obedient to thy Sire.

(Chorus of Bards without.)

Glory, all glory, on *Ayus* attending,
Still in the son may the father we trace;
Justice and valour together extending
The sway of his sceptre and fame of his race—

* As *Yuva rajá*—Young King or Cæsar.

† The stage directions in the original are not more explicit, and the comment is silent.

Son of the monarch the universe filling,
Son of the God of the mist-shedding night,
Son of the sage,* whom the great *Brahma* willing
Called with creation to life and to light.

Second Chorus.

Long may the Goddess of Glory emblazon.
The diadem raised by your father to fame.
Long may the world be delighted to gaze on
The fortune allied to your merit and name.
Long may the halo of *Lakshmi*† clear glowing
Shoot round you its splendors unclouded and wide;
Like *Ganga* from snow crested pinnacles flowing
And rolling majestic to Ocean's far tide.

Rem. (*To Urvasi.*) No ordinary fate dear Sister blesses you
With such a son and Lord.

Urv. I own my happiness.
Come my dear child and offer to the queen,
Your elder mother, filial homage.

Pur. Hold
One moment: we will presently together.

Nar. The splendours of your son's inauguration
Bring to my memory the glorious time
When *Mahasêna* was anointed chief
Of all the heavenly hosts.

Pur. To you I owe

* Or the son of *Pururavas*, the son of *Buddha*, the son of *Chandra* or the moon, the son of the sage *Atri* one of the will—engendered sons of the creator *Brahmá*.

† The goddess of Prosperity Wealth and Power.

‡ *Kártikeya*, the Son of *Siva*, who shortly after his birth was appointed general of the armies of heaven, against the *Daityas* or *Tiany* under *Táraka*.

Such honour.

Nar. Is there ought else, *Indra* can do

To serve his friend.

Pur. To hold me in esteem

Is all I covet—yet haply may this chance—

May learning and prosperity oppose

No more each other, as their wont, as foes:

But in a friendly bond together twined

Ensure the real welfare of mankind.*

[*Exeunt all.*

* A singular but characteristic concluding benediction; one copy adds a stanza desiderative of universal prosperity but it does not occur in another. It may be here observed that the translation has been made from two copies of the text, and one of the comment, all of them full of blunders: the sense has therefore often been made out conjecturally.

If it was necessary to peruse the preceding drama with a liberal allowance for national peculiarities, it is equally requisite in the present instance to adapt our faith to the national creed, and to recognise, for poetical and dramatic purposes, the creations of the mythology of the Hindus.

In this respect, however, no very violent demand is made upon our imagination, as we have none of the monstrous extravagances of the system forced upon our credulity. The intercourse of heroes and of goddesses is the familiar theme of our youthful studies, and the transformation of *Urvasí* into a vine, is not without abundant paralells in the metamorphoses of Ovid. The personages and situations of the superhuman portion of the Drama are both elegant and picturesque, and the grouping of the Nymphs upon the peaks of the Himálaya, or the descent of *Náreda* through the fields of ether, might be represented with as much beauty as facility by the splendid machinery of the theatres of Europe.

There is also a peculiarity in the mythos of this Drama which identifies it with the dramatic compositions of antiquity. Trivial as the incidents may appear, unimportant as may be the loves of the hero and the heroine, both persons and events are subject to an awful control, whose interference invests them with a dignity superior to their natural level. FATE is the ruling principle of the narrative ; and the monarch and the nymph and the Sovereign of the gods himself, are pourtrayed as subject to the inscrutable and inevitable decrees of Destiny.

The simplicity of the story does not admit of much display of character, but the timid constancy of *Urvasí* is not unhappily contrasted with the irresolute haughtiness of the Queen : the Poet too has shewn himself not unacquainted with the springs of human feelings, and his observations, that the husband who is unfaithful, is most profuse in his professions of regard, and that women are too sagacious to mistake counterfeit for genuine affection, are equally shrewd and just.

The chief charm of this piece, however is its poetry : the story, the situations and the characters are all highly imaginative and nothing, if partiality for his work does not mislead the translator, can surpass the beauty and justice of many of the thoughts. To select one as an example were to disparage a number of other passages, and they may be left to the critical acumen and taste of the Reader.